POEMS HERE AT HOME

Other Books by

James Whitcomb Riley.

NEIGHBORLY POEMS.

SKETCHES IN PROSE AND OCCASIONAL VERSES.

AFTERWHILES.

PIPES O' PAN (Prose and Verse).

RHYMES OF CHILDHOOD.

FLYING ISLANDS OF THE NIGHT.

OLD-FASHIONED ROSES (English Edition).

GREEN FIELDS AND RUNNING BROOKS.

(SEE PAGE 18.)

POEMS HERE AT HOME

BY

JAMES WHITCOMB RILEY

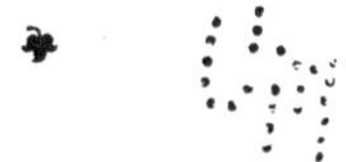

PICTURES BY E. W. KEMBLE

NEW YORK
THE CENTURY CO.
1893

THE DE VINNE PRESS.

TO

MY FATHER

PROEM

The Poems here at Home!—Who 'll write 'em down,
Jes' as they air—in Country and in Town?—
Sowed thick as clods is 'crost the fields and lanes,
Er these-'ere little hop-toads when it rains!—
Who 'll "voice" 'em? as I heerd a feller say
'At speechified on Freedom, t' other day,
And soared the Eagle tel, it 'peared to me,
She was n't bigger 'n a bumble-bee!

Who 'll sort 'em out and set 'em down, says I,
'At 's got a stiddy hand enough to try
To do 'em jestice 'thout a-foolin' some,
And headin' facts off when they want to come?—
Who 's got the lovin' eye, and heart, and brain
To recko'nize 'at nothin 's made in vain—
'At the Good Bein' made the bees and birds
And brutes first choice, and us-folks afterwards?

What We want, as I sense it, in the line
O' poetry is somepin' Yours and Mine—
Somepin' with live-stock in it, and out-doors,
And old crick-bottoms, snags, and sycamores:
Putt weeds in—pizenvines, and underbresh,
As well as johnny-jump-ups, all so fresh
And sassy-like!—and groun'-squir'ls,—yes, and "We,"
As sayin' is,—"We, Us and Company!"

Putt in old Nature's sermonts,—them 's the best,—
And 'casion'ly hang up a hornets' nest
'At boys 'at 's run away from school can git
At handy-like—and let 'em tackle it!
Let us be wrought on, of a truth, to feel
Our proneness fer to hurt more than we heal,
In ministratin' to our vain delights—
Fergittin' even insec's has their rights!

No "Ladies' Amaranth," ner "Treasury" book—
Ner "Night Thoughts," nuther—ner no "Lally Rook"!
We want some poetry 'at 's to Our taste,
Made out o' truck 'at 's jes' a-goin' to waste
'Cause smart folks thinks it 's altogether too
Outrageous common—'cept fer me and you!—
Which goes to argy, all sich poetry
Is 'bliged to rest its hopes on You and Me.

CONTENTS

WHEN SHE COMES HOME

WHEN she comes home again! A thousand ways
I fashion, to myself, the tenderness
Of my glad welcome: I shall tremble—yes;
And touch her, as when first in the old days
I touched her girlish hand, nor dared upraise
Mine eyes, such was my faint heart's sweet distress.
Then silence: and the perfume of her dress:
The room will sway a little, and a haze
Cloy eyesight—soulsight, even—for a space;
And tears—yes; and the ache here in the throat,
To know that I so ill deserve the place
Her arms make for me; and the sobbing note
I stay with kisses, ere the tearful face
Again is hidden in the old embrace.

NOTHIN' TO SAY

NOTHIN' to say, my daughter! Nothin' at all to say!
Gyrls that 's in love, I 've noticed, giner'ly has their way!
Yer mother did, afore you, when her folks objected to me —
Yit here I am and here you air! and yer mother — where is she?

You look lots like yer mother: purty much same in size;
And about the same complected; and favor about the eyes:
Like her, too, about livin' here, because *she* could n't stay;
It 'll 'most seem like you was dead like her! — but I hain't got nothin' to say!

She left you her little Bible — writ yer name acrost the page —
And left her ear-bobs fer you, ef ever you come of age;
I 've alluz kep' 'em and gyuarded 'em, but ef yer goin' away —
Nothin' to say, my daughter! Nothin' at all to say!

You don't rickollect her, I reckon? No; you was n't a year old then!
And now yer — how old *air* you? W'y, child, not "*twenty*"! When?
And yer nex' birthday 's in Aprile? and you want to git married that day?
I wisht yer mother was livin'! — but I hain't got nothin' to say!

Twenty year! and as good a gyrl as parent ever found!
There 's a straw ketched onto yer dress there — I 'll bresh it off — turn round.
(Her mother was jest twenty when us two run away.)
Nothin' to say, my daughter! Nothin' at all to say!

THE ABSENCE OF LITTLE WESLEY

SENCE little Wesley went, the place seems all so strange and still—
W'y, I miss his yell o' "Gran'pap!" as I 'd miss the whipperwill!
And to think I ust to *scold* him fer his everlastin' noise,
When I on'y rickollect him as the best o' little boys!
I wisht a hunderd times a day 'at he 'd come trompin' in,
And all the noise he ever made was twic't as loud ag'in!—
It 'u'd seem like some soft music played on some fine insturment,
'Longside o' this loud lonesomeness, sence little Wesley went!

Of course the clock don't tick no louder than it ust
to do—
Yit now they 's times it 'pears like it 'u'd bu'st
itse'f in two!
And let a rooster, suddent-like, crow som'ers clos't
around,
And seems 's ef, mighty nigh it, it 'u'd lift me off the
ground!
And same with all the cattle when they bawl around
the bars,
In the red o' airly mornin', er the dusk and dew and
stars,
When the neighbers' boys 'at passes never stop, but
jes' go on,
A-whistlin' kind o' to theirse'v's—sence little Wesley 's
gone!

And then, o' nights, when Mother 's settin' up on-
common late,
A-bilin' pears er somepin', and I set and smoke and wait,
Tel the moon out through the winder don't look
bigger 'n a dime,
And things keeps gittin' stiller—stiller—stiller all the
time,—

I 've ketched myse'f a-wishin' like — as I clumb on the cheer
To wind the clock, as I hev done fer more 'n fifty year —
A-wishin' 'at the time hed come fer us to go to bed,
With our last prayers, and our last tears, sence little Wesley 's dead!

THE USED-TO-BE

BEYOND the purple, hazy trees
Of summer's utmost boundaries;
Beyond the sands—beyond the seas—
Beyond the range of eyes like these,
  And only in the reach of the
  Enraptured gaze of Memory,
  There lies a land, long lost to me,—
    The land of Used-to-be!

A land enchanted—such as swung
In golden seas when sirens clung
Along their dripping brinks, and sung
To Jason in that mystic tongue
  That dazed men with its melody—
  O such a land, with such a sea
  Kissing its shores eternally,
    Is the fair Used-to-be.

A land where music ever girds
The air with belts of singing-birds,

And sows all sounds with such sweet words,
That even in the low of herds
  A meaning lives so sweet to me,
  Lost laughter ripples limpidly
  From lips brimmed over with the glee
    Of rare old Used-to-be.

Lost laughter, and the whistled tunes
Of boyhood's mouth of crescent runes,
That rounded, through long afternoons,
To serenading plenilunes—
  When starlight fell so mistily
  That, peering up from bended knee,
  I dreamed 't was bridal drapery
    Snowed over Used-to-be.

O land of love and dreamy thoughts,
And shining fields, and shady spots
Of coolest, greenest grassy plots,
Embossed with wild forget-me-nots!—
  And all ye blooms that longingly
  Lift your fair faces up to me
  Out of the past, I kiss in ye
    The lips of Used-to-be.

AT "THE LITERARY"

FOLKS in town, I reckon, thinks
They git all the fun they air
Runnin' loose 'round!—but, 'y jinks!
We' got fun, and fun to spare,
Right out here amongst the ash-
And oak-timber ever'where!
Some folks else kin cut a dash
'Sides town-people, don't fergit!—
'Specially in *winter*-time,
When they 's snow, and roads is fit.
In them circumstances I 'm
Resig-nated to my lot—
Which putts me in mind o' what
'S called "The Literary."

Us folks in the country sees
Lots o' fun!—Take spellin'-school;
Er ole hoe-down jamborees;
Er revivals; er ef you 'll
Tackle taffy-pullin's you
Kin git fun, and quite a few!—
Same with huskin's. But all these
Kind o' frolics they hain't new
By a hunderd year' er two,
Cipher on it as you please!
But I 'll tell you what I jest
Think walks over all the rest—
Anyway it suits *me* best,—
    That 's "The Literary."

First they started it—"'y gee!"
Thinks-says-I, "this settle-ment
'S gittin' too high-toned fer me!"
But when all begin to jine,
And I heerd *Izory* went,
I jest kind o' drapped in line,
Like you 've seen some sandy, thin,
Scrawny shoat putt fer the crick
Down some pig-trail through the thick

Spice-bresh, where the whole drove 's been
'Bout six weeks 'fore he gits in!—
"Can't tell nothin'," I-says-ee,
"'Bout it tel you go and see
Their blame 'Literary'!"

Very first night I was there
I was 'p'inted to be what
They call "Critic"—so 's a fair
And square jedgment could be got
On the pieces 'at was read,
And on the debate,—"Which air
Most destructive element,

Fire er worter?" Then they hed
Compositions on "Content,"
"Death," and "Botany"; and Tomps

He read one on "Dreenin' swamps"
I p'nounced the boss, and said,
"*So* fur, 'at 's the best thing read
In yer 'Literary'!"

Then they *sung* some — tel I called
Order, and got back ag'in
In the critic's cheer, and hauled
All o' the p'formers in : —
Mandy Brizendine read one
I fergit ; and Doc's was " Thought " ;

And Sarepty's, hern was "None
Air denied 'at knocks;" and Daut—
Fayette Strawnse's little niece—
She got up and spoke a piece:
Then Izory she read hern—
"Best thing in the whole concern,"
I-says-ee; "now le' 's adjourn
This-here 'Literary'!"

They was some contendin'—yit
We broke up in harmony.
Road outside as white as grit,
And as slick as slick could be!—
I 'd fetched 'Zory in my sleigh,—
And I had a heap to say,

Drivin' back—in fact, I driv
'Way around the old north way,
Where the Daubenspeckses live.
'Zory allus—'fore that night—
Never 'peared to feel jest right
In my company.—You see,
On'y thing on earth saved me
    Was that "Literary"!

ONE AFTERNOON

BELOW, cool grasses: over us
The maples waver tremulous.

A slender overture above,
Low breathing as a sigh of love

At first, then gradually strong
And stronger: 't is the locust's song,

Swoln midway to a pæan of glee,
And lost in silence dwindlingly.

Not utter silence; nay, for hid
In ghosts of it, the katydid

Chirrs a diluted echo of
The loveless song he makes us love.

The low boughs are drugged heavily
With shade; the poem you read to me

Is not more gracious than the trill
Of birds that twitter as they will.

Half consciously, with upturned eyes,
I hear your voice — I see the skies,

Where, o'er bright rifts, the swallows glance
Like glad thoughts o'er a countenance;

And voices near and far are blent
Like sweet chords of some instrument

Awakened by the trembling touch
Of hands that love it overmuch.

Dear heart, let be the book awhile!
I want your face — I want your smile!

Tell me how gladder now are they
Who look on us from heaven to-day.

DOWN TO THE CAPITAL

I ' BE'N down to the Capital at Washington, D. C.,
Where Congerss meets and passes on the pensions ort to be
Allowed to old one-legged chaps, like me, 'at sence the war
Don't wear their pants in pairs at all — and yit how proud we are!

Old Flukens, from our deestrick, jes' turned in and tuck and made
Me stay with him while I was there; and longer 'at I stayed
The more I kep' a-wantin' jes' to kind o' git away,
And yit a-feelin' sociabler with Flukens ever' day.

You see I 'd got the idy — and I guess most folks
agrees —
'At men as rich as him, you know, kin do jes' what
they please;
A man worth stacks o' money, and a Congerssman
and all,
And livin' in a buildin' bigger 'n Masonic Hall!

Now mind, I 'm not a-faultin' Fluke — he made his
money square:
We both was Forty-niners, and both bu'sted gittin'
there;
I weakened and onwindlassed, and he stuck and
stayed and made
His millions; don't know what *I 'm* worth untel my
pension 's paid.

But I was goin' to tell you — er a-ruther goin' to try
To tell you how he 's livin' now: gas burnin' mighty
nigh
In ever' room about the house; and all the night,
about,
Some blame reception goin' on, and money goin' out.

They 's people there from all the world — jes' ever' kind 'at lives,
Injuns and all! and Senaters, and Ripresentatives;
And girls, you know, jes' dressed in gauze and roses, I *de*clare,
And even old men shamblin' round and waltzin' with 'em there!

And bands a-tootin' circus-tunes, 'way in some other room
Jes' chokin' full o' hot-house plants and pinies and perfume;
And fountains, squirtin' stiddy all the time; and statutes, made
Out o' puore marble, 'peared-like, sneakin' round there in the shade.

And Fluke he coaxed and begged and pled with *me* to take a hand
And sashay in amongst 'em — crutch and all, you understand;
But when I said how tired I was, and made fer open air,
He follered, and tel five o'clock we set a-talkin' there.

"My God!" says he — Fluke says to me, "I 'm
tireder 'n you;
Don't putt up yer tobacker tel you give a man a chew.
Set back a leetle furder in the shadder — that 'll do;
I 'm tireder 'n you, old man; I 'm tireder 'n you.

"You see that-air old dome," says he, "humped up
ag'inst the sky?
It 's grand, first time you see it; but it changes, by
and by,
And then it stays jes' thataway — jes' anchored high
and dry
Betwixt the sky up yender and the achin' of yer
eye.

"Night 's purty; not so purty, though, as what it
ust to be
When my first wife was livin'. You remember her?"
says he.
I nodded-like, and Fluke went on, "I wonder now
ef she
Knows where I am — and what I am — and what
I ust to be?

"That band in there! — I ust to think 'at music could n't wear
A feller out the way it does; but that ain't music there —
That 's jes' a' *imitation*, and like ever'thing, I swear,
I hear, er see, er tetch, er taste, er tackle anywhere!

"It 's all jes' *artificial*, this-ere high-priced life of ours;
The theory, *it 's* sweet enough, tel it saps down and sours.
They 's no *home* left, ner *ties* o' home about it. By the powers,
The whole thing 's artificialer 'n artificial flowers!

"And all I want, and could lay down and *sob* fer, is to know
The homely things of homely life; fer instance, jes' to go
And set down by the kitchen stove — Lord! that 'u'd rest me so,—
Jes' set there, like I ust to do, and laugh and joke, you know.

"Jes' set there, like I ust to do," says Fluke, a-startin' in,
'Peared-like, to say the whole thing over to his-se'f ag'in;
Then stopped and turned, and kind o' coughed, and stooped and fumbled fer
Somepin' o' 'nuther in the grass—I guess his hand-kercher.

Well, sence I 'm back from Washington, where I left Fluke a-still
A-leggin' fer me, heart and soul, on that-air pen-sion bill,
I 've half-way struck the notion, when I think o' wealth and sich,
They 's nothin' much patheticker 'n jes' a-bein' rich!

THE POET OF THE FUTURE

O THE Poet of the Future! He will come to us as comes
The beauty of the bugle's voice above the roar of drums —
The beauty of the bugle's voice above the roar and din
Of battle-drums that pulse the time the victor marches in.
His hands will hold no harp, in sooth; his lifted brow will bear
No coronet of laurel — nay, nor symbol anywhere,
Save that his palms are brothers to the toiler's at the plow,
His face to heaven, and the dew of duty on his brow.

He will sing across the meadow,—and the woman at the well
Will stay the dripping bucket, with a smile ineffable;

And the children in the orchard will gaze wistfully the
way
The happy song comes to them, with the fragrance of
the hay;
The barn will neigh in answer, and the pasture-lands
behind
Will chime with bells, and send responsive lowings
down the wind;
And all the echoes of the wood will jubilantly call
In sweetest mimicry of that one sweetest voice of all.

O the Poet of the Future! He will come as man to
man,
With the honest arm of labor, and the honest face of
tan,
The honest heart of lowliness, the honest soul of love
For human-kind and nature-kind about him and above.
His hands will hold no harp, in sooth; his lifted brow
will bear
No coronet of laurel—nay, nor symbol anywhere,
Save that his palms are brothers to the toiler's at the
plow,
His face to heaven, and the dew of duty on his brow.

THE OLD MAN AND JIM

Old man never had much to say—
  'Ceptin' to Jim,—
And Jim was the wildest boy he had—
  And the old man jes' wrapped up in him!
Never heerd him speak but once
Er twice in my life,—and first time was
When the army broke out, and Jim he went,
The old man backin' him, fer three months;
An' all 'at I heerd the old man say
Was, jes' as we turned to start away,—
  "Well, good-by, Jim:
    Take keer of yourse'f!"

'Peared-like, he was more satisfied
  Jes' *lookin'* at Jim
And likin' him all to hisse'f-like, see?—
  'Cause he was jes' wrapped up in him!

And over and over I mind the day
The old man come and stood round in the
    way
While we was drillin', a-watchin' Jim—
And down at the deepot a-heerin' him say,
  "Well, good-by, Jim:
    Take keer of yourse'f!"

Never was nothin' about the *farm*
  Disting'ished Jim;
Neighbors all ust to wonder why
  The old man 'peared wrapped up in him:
But when Cap. Biggler he writ back
'At Jim was the bravest boy we had
In the whole dern rigiment, white er black,
And his fightin' good as his farmin' bad—
'At he had led, with a bullet clean
Bored through his thigh, and carried the flag
Through the bloodiest battle you ever seen,—
The old man wound up a letter to him
'At Cap. read to us, 'at said: "Tell Jim
    Good-by,
    And take keer of hisse'f."

Jim come home jes' long enough
  To take the whim
'At he 'd like to go back in the calvery—
  And the old man jes' wrapped up in him!
Jim 'lowed 'at he 'd had sich luck afore,
Guessed he 'd tackle her three years more.
And the old man give him a colt he 'd raised,
And follered him over to Camp Ben Wade,
And laid around fer a week er so,
Watchin' Jim on dress-parade—
Tel finally he rid away,
And last he heerd was the old man say,—
  "Well, good-by, Jim:
    Take keer of yourse'f!"

Tuk the papers, the old man did,
  A-watchin' fer Jim—
Fully believin' he 'd make his mark
  Some way—jes' wrapped up in him!—
And many a time the word 'u'd come
'At stirred him up like the tap of a drum—
At Petersburg, fer instunce, where
Jim rid right into their cannons there,

And *tuk* 'em, and p'inted 'em t' other way,
And socked it home to the boys in gray,
As they scooted fer timber, and on and on —
Jim a lieutenant and one arm gone,
And the old man's words in his mind all day,—
  "Well, good-by, Jim:
    Take keer of yourse'f!"

Think of a private, now, perhaps,
  We 'll say like Jim,
'At 's clumb clean up to the shoulder-straps —
  And the old man jes' wrapped up in him!
Think of him — with the war plum' through,
And the glorious old Red-White-and-Blue
A-laughin' the news down over Jim,
And the old man, bendin' over him —
The surgeon turnin' away with tears
'At had n't leaked fer years and years,
As the hand of the dyin' boy clung to
His father's, the old voice in his ears,—
  "Well, good-by, Jim:
    Take keer of yourse'f!"

THOUGHTS ON THE LATE WAR

I WAS for Union — you, ag'in' it.
'Pears like, to me, each side was winner,
Lookin' at now and all 'at 's in it.
Le' 's go to dinner.

Le' 's kind o' jes' set down together
And do some pardnership forgittin'—
Talk, say, fer instunce, 'bout the weather,
Er somepin' fittin'.

The war, you know, 's all done and ended,
And ain't changed no p'ints o' the compass;
Both North and South the health 's jes' splendid
As 'fore the rumpus.

The old farms and the old plantations
Still ockipies the'r old positions.
Le' 's git back to old situations
And old ambitions.

Le' 's let up on this blame', infernal
Tongue-lashin' and lap-jacket vauntin',
And git back home to the eternal
Ca'm we 're a-wantin'.

Peace kind o' sort o' suits my diet —
When women does my cookin' for me.
Ther' was n't overly much pie et
Durin' the army.

THE OLD BAND

It 's mighty good to git back to the old town, shore,
Considerin' I 've be'n away twenty year and more.
Sence I moved then to Kansas, of course I see a change,
A-comin' back, and notice things that 's new to me and strange;
Especially at evening when yer new band-fellers meet,
In fancy uniforms and all, and play out on the street—
. . What 's come of old Bill Lindsey and the saxhorn fellers—say?
I want to hear the *old* band play.

What 's come of Eastman, and Nat Snow? And
where 's War Barnett at?
And Nate and Bony Meek; Bill Hart; Tom Richa'-
son and that
Air brother of him played the drum as twic't as big
as Jim;
And old Hi Kerns, the carpenter — say, what 's be-
come o' him?
I make no doubt yer *new band* now 's a *competenter*
band,
And plays their music more by note than what they
play by hand,
And stylisher and grander tunes; but somehow —
*any*way,
I want to hear the *old* band play.

Sich tunes as "John Brown's Body" and "Sweet
Alice," don't you know;
And "The Camels is A-comin'," and "John Ander-
son, my Jo";
And a dozent others of 'em — "Number Nine" and
"Number 'Leven"
Was favo-*rites* that fairly made a feller dream o'
heaven.

And when the boys 'u'd saranade, I 've laid so still
in bed
I 've even heerd the locus'-blossoms droppin' on the
shed
When "Lily Dale," er "Hazel Dell," had sobbed
and died away —
. . . I want to hear the *old* band play.

Yer *new* band ma'by beats it, but the *old band* 's
what I said —
It allus 'peared to kind o' chord with somepin' in my
head;
And, whilse I 'm no musicianer, when my blame' eyes
is jes'
Nigh drownded out, and Mem'ry squares her jaws
and sort o' says
She *won't* ner *never will* fergit, I want to jes' turn in
And take and light right out o' here and git back
West ag'in
And *stay* there, when I git there, where I never haf'
to say
I want to hear the *old* band play.

" LAST CHRISTMAS WAS A YEAR AGO "

(THE OLD LADY SPEAKS)

LAST Christmas was a year ago,
Says I to David, I-says-I,
"We 're goin' to morning-service, so
You hitch up right away : I 'll try
To tell the girls jes' what to do
Fer dinner.—We 'll be back by two."
I did n't wait to hear what he
Would more 'n like say back to me,
But banged the stable door and flew
Back to the house, jes' plumb chilled through.

Cold! *Wooh!* how cold it was! My-oh!
Frost flyin', and the air, you know,
" Jes' sharp enough," heerd David swear,
" To shave a man and cut his hair!"

And blow and blow! and snow and snow!—
Where it had drifted 'long the fence
And 'crost the road,— some places, though,
Jes' swep' clean to the gravel, so
The goin' was as bad fer sleighs
As 't was fer wagons,— and both ways,
'Twixt snowdrifts and the bare ground, I 've
Jes' wundered we got through alive;
I hain't saw nothin', 'fore er sence,
'At beat it anywheres, I know—
Last Christmas was a year ago.

And David said, as we set out,
'At Christmas services was 'bout
As cold and wuthless kind o' love
To offer up as he knowed of;
And as fer him, he railly thought
'At the Good Bein' up above
Would think more of us — as he ought—
A-stayin' home on sich a day,
And thankin' of him thataway!
And jawed on, in an undertone,
'Bout leavin' Lide and Jane alone

There on the place, and me not there
To oversee 'em, and p'pare
The stuffin' fer the turkey and
The sass and all, you understand.

I 've allus managed David by
Jes' sayin' *nothin'*. That was why
He 'd chased Lide's beau away—'cause
Lide
She 'd allus take up Perry's side
When David tackled him; and so,
Last Christmas was a year ago,—
Er ruther, 'bout *a week afore*,—
David and Perry 'd quarr'l'd about
Some tom-fool argyment, you know,
And Pap told him to "Jes' git out
O' there, and not to come no more,
And, when he went, to shet the door!"
And as he passed the winder, we
Saw Perry, white as white could be,
March past, onhitch his hoss, and light
A see-gyar, and lope out o' sight.
Then Lide she come to me and cried!
And I said nothin'—was no need.

And yit, you know, that man jes' got
Right out o' there 's ef he 'd be'n shot,
P'tendin' he must go and feed
The stock er somepin'. Then I tried
To git the pore girl pacified.

But, gittin' back to — where was we ? —
Oh, yes ! — where David lectered me
All way to meetin', high and low,
Last Christmas was a year ago :
Fer all the awful cold, they was
A fair attendunce ; mostly, though,
The crowd was 'round the stoves, you see,
Thawin' their heels and scrougin' us.
Ef 't 'ad n't be'n fer the old Squire
Givin' *his* seat to us, as in
We stomped, a-fairly perishin',
And David could 'a' got no fire,
He 'd jes' 'a' drapped there in his tracks :
And Squire, as I was tryin' to yit
Make room fer him, says, "No ; the fac's
Is, *I* got to git up and git
'*Ithout* no preachin'. Jes' got word —
'Trial fer life — can't be deferred!"

And out he putt! And all way through
The sermont — and a long one, too —
I could n't he'p but think o' Squire
And us changed round so, and admire
His gintle ways,— to give his warm
Bench up, and have to face the storm.
And when I noticed David, he
Was needin' jabbin'— I thought best
To kind o' sort o' let him rest:
'Peared-like he slep' so peacefully!
And then I thought o' home, and how
And what the gyrls was doin' now,
And kind o' prayed, 'way in my breast,
And breshed away a tear er two
As David waked, and church was through.

By time we 'd "howdyed" round and shuck
Hands with the neighbers, must 'a' tuck
A half hour longer: ever' one
A-sayin' "Christmas gift!" afore
David er me — so we got none!
But David warmed up, more and more,
And got so jokey-like, and had
His sperits up, and 'peared so glad,

I whispered to him, "S'pose you ast
A passel of 'em come and eat
Their dinners with us. Gyrls 's got
A full-and-plenty fer the lot
And all their kin!" So David passed
The invite round: and ever' seat
In ever' wagon-bed and sleigh
Was jes' packed, as we rode away,—
The young folks, mild er so along,
A-strikin' up a sleighin'-song,
Tel David laughed and yelled, you know,
And jes' whirped up and sent the snow
And gravel flyin' thick and fast—
Last Christmas was a year ago.
W'y, that-air seven-mild ja'nt we come—
Jes' seven mild scant from church to home—
It did n't 'pear, *that* day, to be
Much furder railly 'n 'bout *three!*

But I was purty squeamish by
The time home hove in sight and I
See two vehickles standin' there
Already. So says I, "*Prepare!*"
All to myse'f. And presently

David he sobered; and says he,
"Hain't that-air Squire Hanch's old
Buggy," he says, "and claybank mare?"
Says I, "Le' 's git in out the cold—
Your company 's nigh 'bout froze!" He says,
"Whose sleigh 's that-air, a-standin' there?"
Says I, "It 's no odds *whose*—*you* jes'
Drive to the house and let us out,
'Cause we 're jes' *freezin'*, nigh about!"
Well, David swung up to the door,
And out we piled. And first I heerd
Jane's voice, then *Lide's*,—I thought afore
I reached that gyrl I 'd jes' die, shore;
And *when* I reached her, would n't keered
Much ef I had, I was so glad,
A-kissin' her through my green veil,
And jes' excitin' her so bad,
'At *she* broke down *herse'f*—and Jane,
She cried—and we all hugged again.
And *David?*—David jes' turned pale!—
Looked at the gyrls, and then at me,
Then at the open door—and then—
"Is old Squire Hanch in there?" says he.

The old Squire suddently stood in
The doorway, with a sneakin' grin.
"Is Perry Anders in there, too?"
Says David, limberin' all through,
As Lide and me both grabbed him, and
Perry stepped out and waved his hand
And says, "Yes, Pap." And David jes'
Stooped and kissed Lide, and says, "I guess
Yer *mother* 's much to blame as you.
Ef *she* kin resk him, I kin too!"

. . . . . .

The dinner we had then hain't no
Bit better 'n the one to-day
'At we 'll have fer 'em. Hear some sleigh
A-jinglin' now. David, fer *me*,
I wish you 'd jes' go out and see
Ef they 're in sight yit. It jes' does
Me good to think, in times like these,
Lide 's done so well. And David, he 's
More tractabler 'n what he was—
Last Christmas was a year ago.

THE ALL-KIND MOTHER

Lo, whatever is at hand
Is full meet for the demand:
Nature ofttimes giveth best
When she seemeth chariest.
She hath shapen shower and sun
To the need of every one—
Summer bland and winter drear,
Dimpled pool and frozen mere.
All thou lackest she hath still
Near thy finding and thy fill.
Yield her fullest faith, and she
Will endow thee royally.

Loveless weed and lily fair
She attendeth, here and there—
Kindly to the weed as to
The lorn lily teared with dew.

Each to her hath use as dear
As the other; an thou clear
Thy cloyed senses thou may'st see
Haply all the mystery.
Thou shalt see the lily get
Its divinest blossom; yet
Shall the weed's tip bloom no less
With the song-bird's gleefulness.

Thou art poor, or thou art rich—
Never lightest matter which;
All the glad gold of the noon,
All the silver of the moon,
She doth lavish on thee, while
Thou withholdest any smile
Of thy gratitude to her,
Baser used than usurer.
Shame be on thee an thou seek
Not her pardon, with hot cheek,
And bowed head, and brimming eyes,
At her merciful "Arise!"

OUR HIRED GIRL

OUR hired girl, she 's 'Lizabuth Ann;
  An' she can cook best things to eat!
She ist puts dough in our pie-pan,
  An' pours in somepin' 'at 's good an' sweet;
An' nen she salts it all on top
With cinnamon; an' nen she 'll stop
  An' stoop an' slide it, ist as slow,
In th' old cook-stove, so 's 't won't slop

An' git all spilled; nen bakes it, so
It 's custard-pie, first thing you know!
An' nen she 'll say,
"Clear out o' my way!
They 's time fer work, an' time fer play!
Take yer dough, an' run, child, run!
Er I cain't git no cookin' done!"

When our hired girl 'tends like she 's mad,
An' says folks got to walk the chalk
When *she 's* around, er wisht they had!
I play out on our porch an' talk
To th' Raggedy Man 'at mows our lawn;
An' he says, "*Whew!*" an' nen leans on
His old crook-scythe, and blinks his eyes,
An' sniffs all 'round an' says, "I swawn!
Ef my old nose don't tell me lies,
It 'pears like I smell custard-pies!"
An' nen *he 'll* say,
"Clear out o' my way!
They 's time fer work, an' time fer play!
Take yer dough, an' run, child, run!
Er she cain't git no cookin' done!"

Wunst our hired girl, when she
  Got the supper, an' we all et,
An' it wuz night, an' Ma an' me
  An' Pa went wher' the "Social" met,—
An' nen when we come home, an' see
A light in the kitchen-door, an' we
  Heerd a maccordeun, Pa says, "Lan'-
O'-Gracious! who can *her* beau be?"
  An' I marched in, an' 'Lizabuth Ann
  Wuz parchin' corn fer the Raggedy Man!
      Better say,
    "Clear out o' the way!
  They 's time fer work, an' time fer play!
    Take the hint, an' run, child, run!
    Er we cain't git no courtin' done!"

THE RAGGEDY MAN

O THE Raggedy Man! He works fer Pa;
An' he 's the goodest man ever you saw!
He comes to our house every day,
An' waters the horses, an' feeds 'em hay;
An' he opens the shed—an' we all ist laugh
When he drives out our little old wobble-ly calf;
An' nen—ef our hired girl says he can—
He milks the cow fer 'Lizabuth Ann.—
  Ain't he a' awful good Raggedy Man?
    Raggedy! Raggedy! Raggedy Man!

W'y, the Raggedy Man—he 's ist so good,
He splits the kindlin' an' chops the wood;
An' nen he spades in our garden, too,
An' does most things 'at *boys* can't do.—
He clumbed clean up in our big tree
An' shooked a' apple down fer me—
An' 'nother 'n', too, fer 'Lizabuth Ann—
An' 'nother 'n', too, fer the Raggedy Man.—
  Ain't he a' awful kind Raggedy Man?
    Raggedy! Raggedy! Raggedy Man!

An' the Raggedy Man, he knows most rhymes,
An' tells 'em, ef I be good, sometimes:
Knows 'bout Giunts, an' Griffuns, an' Elves,
An' the Squidgicum-Squees 'at swallers therselves!
An', wite by the pump in our pasture-lot,
He showed me the hole 'at the Wunks is got,
'At lives 'way deep in the ground, an' can
Turn into me, er 'Lizabuth Ann!
  Ain't he a funny old Raggedy Man?
    Raggedy! Raggedy! Raggedy Man!

The Raggedy Man—one time, when he
Wuz makin' a little bow'-n'-orry fer me,
Says, "When you 're big like your Pa is,
Air *you* go' to keep a fine store like his—
An' be a rich merchunt—an' wear fine clothes?—
Er what *air* you go' to be, goodness knows?"
An' nen he laughed at 'Lizabuth Ann,
An' I says, "'M go' to be a Raggedy Man!—
  I 'm ist go' to be a nice Raggedy Man!"
    Raggedy! Raggedy! Raggedy Man!

GOIN' TO THE FAIR

(OLD STYLE)

WHEN Me an' my Ma an' Pa went to the Fair,
Ma borried Mizz Rollins-uz rigg to go there,
'Cause *our* buggy 's *new*, an' Ma says, "Mercy-sake!
It would n't hold *half* the folks *she 's* go' to take!"
An' she took Marindy, an' Jane's twins, an' Jo,
An' Aunty Van Meters-uz girls — an' old Slo'
Magee, 'at 's so fat, come a-scrougin' in there,
When me an' my Ma an' Pa went to the Fair!

The road 's full o' loads-full 'ist ready to bust,
An' all hot, an' smokin' an' chokin' with dust;
The Wolffs an' their wagon, an' Brizentines, too —
An' horses 'ist r'ared when the toot-cars come through!
An' 'way from fur off we could hear the band play,
An' peoples all there 'u'd 'ist whoop an' hooray!
An' I stood on the dash-board, an' Pa boost me there
'Most high as the fence, when we went to the Fair!

An' when we 'uz there an' inside, we could see
Wher' the flag 's on a pole wher' a show 's go' to be;
An' boys up in trees, an' the grea'-big balloon
'At did n't goned up a-tall, all afternoon!
An' a man in the crowd there gived money away —
An' Pa says "*he* 'd ruther earn *his* by the day!"—
An' *he* gim-me some, an' says "ain't nothin' there
Too good fer his boy," when we went to the Fair!

Wisht the Raggedy Man wuz there, too! — but he
says,
"Don't talk fairs to *me*, child! I went to one; —
yes,—
An' they wuz a swing there ye rode — an' I rode,
An' a thing-um-a-jing 'at ye blowed — an' I blowed;
An' they wuz a game 'at ye played — an' I played,
An' a hitch in the same wher' ye paid — an' I paid;
An' they wuz *two* bad to one good peoples there —
Like *you* an' your *Pa* an' Ma went to the Fair!"

GLADNESS

My ole man named Silas: he
Dead long 'fo' ole Gin'l Lee
S'rendah, whense de wah wuz done.
Yanks dey tuk de plantation —
Mos' high-handed evah you see! —
Das rack roun', an' fiah an' bu'n,
An' jab de beds wid deir bay'net-gun,
An' sweah we niggahs all scotch-free,—
An' Massah John C. Pemberton
    Das tuk an' run!

"Gord Armighty, marm," he 'low,
"He'p you an' de chillen now!"
Blaze crack out 'n de roof inside
Tel de big house all das charified!
Smoke roll out 'n de ole hay-mow
An' de wa'house do' — an' de fiah das roah —

An' all dat 'backer, 'bout half dried,
Hit smell das fried!

Nelse, my ol'est boy, an' John,—
Atter de baby das wuz bo'n,
Erlongse dem times, an' lak ter 'a' died,
An' Silas he be'n slip an' gone
'Bout eight weeks ter de Union side,—
Dem two boys dey start fo' ter fine
An' jine deir fader acrost de line.
Ovahseeah he wade an' tromp
Eveh-which-way fo' to track 'em down—
Sic de bloodhoun' fro' de swamp—
An' bring de news dat John he drown'—
But dey save de houn'!

Someway ner Nelse git fro'
An' fight fo' de ole Red, White, an' Blue,
Lak his fader is, ter er heart's delight—
An' nen crope back wid de news, one night—
Sayes, "Fader 's killed in a scrimmage-fight,
An' saunt farewell ter ye all, an' sayes
Fo' ter name de baby 'Gladness,' 'caze

Mighty nigh she 'uz be'n borned free!"
An' de boy he smile so strange at me
I sayes, "Yo' 's hurt *yo'se'f!*" an' he
Sayes, "I 's killed, too — an' dat 's all else!"
  An' dah lay Nelse!

Hope an' Angrish, de twins, be'n sole
'Fo' dey mo' 'n twelve year ole:
An' Mary Magdaline sole too.
An' dah I 's lef', wid Knox-Andrew,
An' Lily, an' Maje, an' Margaret,
An' little gal-babe, 'at 's borned dat new
She scaisely ole fo' ter be named yet —
Less 'n de name 'at Si say to —
  An' co'se hit *do*.

An' I taken dem chillen, evah one
(An' a-oh my Mastah's will be done!),
An' I break fo' de Norf, whah dey all raised free
(An' a-oh good Mastah, come git me!).
Knox-Andrew, on de day he died,
Lef' his fambly er shop an' er lot berside;
An' Maje die ownin' er team — an' he
  Lef' all ter me.

Lily she work at de Gran' Hotel —
(Mastah! Mastah! take me — do!) —
An' Lily she ain' married well:
He stob a man — an' she die too;
An' Margaret she too full er pride
Ter own her kin tel er day she died!
But Gladness! — 't ain' soun' sho'-nuff true, —
But she teached school! — an' er white folks,
Ruspec' dat gal 'mos' high ez I do! —
'Caze she 'uz de bes' an de mos' high bred —
De las' chile bo'n, an' de las' chile dead,
O' all ten head!

. . . . . .

Gladness! Gladness! a-oh my chile!
Wa'm my soul in yo' sweet smile!
Daughter o' Silas! o-rise an' sing
Tel er heart-beat pat lak er pigeon-wing!
Sayes, O Gladness! wake dem eyes —
Sayes, a-lif' dem folded han's, an' rise —
Sayes, a-coax me erlong ter Paradise,
An' a-hail de King,
O Gladness!

FESSLER'S BEES

"TALKIN' 'bout yer bees," says Ike,
Speakin' slow and ser'ous-like,
"D' ever tell you 'bout old 'Bee'—
Old 'Bee' Fessler?" Ike says-he!
"Might call him a *bee-expert*,
When it come to handlin' bees,—
Roll the sleeves up of his shirt
And wade in amongst the trees
Where a swarm 'u'd settle, and—
Blamedest man on top of dirt!—
Rake 'em with his naked hand
Right back in the hive ag'in,
Jes' as easy as you please!
Nary bee 'at split the breeze
Ever jabbed a stinger in
Old 'Bee' Fessler—jes' in fun,
Er in *airnest*—nary one!—
Could n't agg one *on* to, nuther,
Ary one way er the other!

"Old 'Bee' Fessler," Ike says-he,
"Made a speshyality
Jes' o' bees; and built a shed—
Len'th about a half a mild!
Had about a *thousan'* head
O' hives, I reckon—tame and wild!
Durndest buzzin' ever wuz—
Wuss 'n telegraph-poles does
When they 're sockin' home the news
Tight as they kin let 'er loose!
Visitors rag out and come
Clean from town to hear 'em hum,
And stop at the kivered bridge;
But wuz some 'u'd cross the ridge
Allus, and go clos'ter—so 's
They could *see* 'em hum, I s'pose!
'Peared-like strangers down that track
Allus met folks comin' back
Lookin' extry fat and hearty
Fer a city picnic party!

"'Fore he went to Floridy,
Old 'Bee' Fessler," Ike says-he—

"Old 'Bee' Fessler could n't bide
Childern on his place," says Ike.
"Yit, fer all, they 'd climb inside
And tromp round there, keerless-like,
In their bare feet. 'Bee' could tell
Ev'ry town-boy by his yell —
So 's 'at when they bounced the fence,
Did n't make no difference!
He 'd jes' git down on one knee
In the grass and pat the bee! —
And, ef 't 'ad n't stayed stuck in,
Fess' 'u'd set the sting ag'in,
'N' potter off, and wait around
Fer the old famillyer sound.
Allus boys there, more er less,
Scootin' round the premises!
When the buckwheat wuz in bloom,
Lawzy! how them bees 'u'd boom
Round the boys 'at crossed that way
Fer the crick on Saturday!
Never seemed to me su'prisin'
'At the sting o' bees 'uz p'izin!

"'Fore he went to Floridy,"
Ike says, "nothin' 'bout a bee

'At old Fessler did n't know,—
W'y, it jes' 'peared-like 'at he
Knowed their language, high and low:
Claimed he told jes' by their buzz
What their wants and wishes wuz!
Peek in them-air little holes
Round the porches o' the hive—
Drat their pesky little souls!—
Could 'a' skinned the man alive!
Bore right in there with his thumb,
And squat down and scrape the gum
Outen ev'ry hole, and blow
'N' bresh the crumbs off, don't you know!
Take the roof off, and slide back
Them-air glass concerns they pack
Full o' honey, and jes' lean
'N' grabble 'mongst 'em fer the queen!
Fetch her out and *show* you to her—
Jes', you might say, *interview* her!

"Year er two," says Ike, says-he,
"'Fore he went to Floridy,
Fessler struck the theory,
Honey was the same as *love*—

You could make it day and night:
Said them bees o' his could be
Got jes' twic't the work out of
Ef a feller managed right.
He contended ef bees found
Blossoms all the year around,
He could git 'em down at once
To work all the *winter* months
Same as *summer*. So, one fall,
When their summer's work wuz done,
'Bee' turns in and robs 'em all;
Loads the hives then, one by one,
On the cyars, and 'lowed he 'd see
Ef bees loafed in *Floridy!*
Said he bet he 'd know the reason
Ef *his* did n't work that season!

"And," says Ike, "it 's jes'," says-he,
"Like old Fessler says to me:
'Any man kin fool a *bee*,
Git him down in Floridy!'
'Peared at fust, as old 'Bee' said,
Fer to kind o' turn their head

Fer a spell; but, bless you! they
Did n't lose a half a day
Altogether! — Jes' lit in
Them-air tropics, and them-air
Cacktusses a-ripen-nin',
'N' magnolyers, and sweet-peas,
'N' 'simmon and pineapple trees,
'N' ripe bananners, here and there,
'N' dates a-danglin' in the breeze,
'N' figs and reezins ev'rywhere,
All waitin' jes' fer Fessler's bees!
'N' Fessler's bees, with gaumy wings,
A-gittin' down and *whoopin'* things! —
Fessler kind o' overseein'
'Em, and sort o' '*hee-o-heein'!*'

"'Fore he went to *Floridy*,
Old 'Bee' Fessler," Ike says-he,
"Wuz n't counted, jes' to say,
Mean er or'n'ry anyway;
On'y ev'ry 'tarnel dime
'At 'u'd pass him on the road
He 'd ketch up with, ev'ry time;
And no mortal ever knowed

Him to spend a copper cent —
'Less on some fool-*'speriment*
With them *bees* — like that-un he
Played on 'em in Floridy.
Fess', of course, *he* tuck his ease,
But 't wuz *bilious* on the bees!
Sweat, you know, 'u'd jes' stand out
On their *forreds* — pant and groan,
And grunt round and limp about! —
And old 'Bee,' o' course, a-knowin'
'T wuz n't no fair shake to play
On them pore dumb insecks, ner
To abuse 'em thataway.
Bees has rights, I 'm here to say,
And that 's all they ast him fer!
Man as mean as *that*, jes' 'pears,
Could 'a' worked bees on the sheers!
Cleared big money — well, I guess,
'Bee' shipped honey, more er less,
Into ev'ry state, perhaps,
Ever putt down in the maps!

"But by time he fetched 'em back
In the spring ag'in," says Ike,

"They wuz actin' s'picious-like:
Though they 'peared to lost the track
O' ev'rything they saw er heard,
They 'd lay round the porch, and gap'
At their shadders in the sun,
Do-less like, ontel some bird
Suddently 'u'd mayby drap
In a bloomin' churry-tree,
Twitterin' a tune 'at run
In their minds familiously!
They 'd revive up, kind o', then,
Like they argied: 'Well, it 's be'n
The most longest summer we
Ever saw er want to see!
Must be *right*, though, er *old 'Bee'*
'U'd notify us!' they says-ee;
And they 'd sort o' square their chin
And git down to work ag'in —
Moanin' round their honey-makin',
Kind o' like their head was achin'.
Tetchin' fer to see how they
Trusted Fessler thataway—
Him a-lazin' round, and smirkin'
To hisse'f to see 'em workin'!

"But old 'Bee,'" says Ike, says-he,—
"*Now* where is he? *Where 's* he gone?
Where 's the head he helt so free?
Where 's his pride and vanity?
What 's his hopes a-restin' on?—
Never knowed a man," says Ike,
"Take advantage of a bee,
'At affliction did n't strike
Round in that vicinity!
Sinners allus suffers some,
And *old Fessler's* reck'nin' come!
That-air man to-day is jes'
Like the grass 'at Scriptur' says
Cometh up, and then turns in
And jes' gits cut down ag'in!
Old 'Bee' Fessler," Ike says-he,
"Says, last fall, says he to me—
'Ike,' says he, 'them bees has jes'
Ciphered out my or'n'riness!
Nary bee in ary swarm
On the whole endurin' farm
Won't have nothin' more to do
With a man as mean as I 've
Be'n to them, last year er two!

Nary bee in ary hive
But 'll turn his face away,
Like they ort, whenever they
Hear my footprints drawin' nigh!'
And old 'Bee,' he 'd sort o' shy
Round oneasy in his cheer,
Wipe his eyes, and yit the sap,
Spite o' all, 'u'd haf' to drap,
As he wound up: 'Would n't keer
Quite so much ef they 'd jes' light
In and settle things up right,
Like they ort; but—blame the thing!—
'Pears-like they won't even *sting!*
Pepper me, the way I felt,
And I 'd thank 'em, ev'ry welt!'
And as miz'able and mean
As 'Bee' looked, ef you 'd 'a' seen
Them-air hungry eyes," says Ike,
"You 'd fergive him, more 'n like.

"Wisht you had 'a' knowed old 'Bee'
'Fore he went to Floridy!"

A LIFE TERM

SHE was false, and he was true,—
  Thus their lives were rent apart;
'T was his dagger driven through
  A mad rival's heart.

He was shut away. The moon
  May not find him; nor the stars—
Nay, nor yet the sun of noon
  Pierce his prison bars.

She was left—again to sin—
  Mistress of all siren arts:
The poor, soulless heroine
  Of a hundred hearts!

Though she dare not think of him
  Who believed her lies, and so
Sent a ghost adown the dim
  Path she dreads to go,—

He, in fancy, smiling, sips
  Of her kisses, purer yet
Than the dew upon the lips
  Of the violet.

"THE LITTLE MAN IN THE TINSHOP"

WHEN I was a little boy, long ago,
And spoke of the theatre as "the show,"
The first one that I went to see,
Mother's brother it was took me—
(My uncle, of course, though he seemed to be
Only a boy—I loved him so!)

And ah, how pleasant he made it all!
And the things he knew that *I* should know!—
The stage, the "drop," and the frescoed wall;
The sudden flash of the lights; and oh,
The orchestra, with its melody,
And the lilt and jingle and jubilee
Of "The Little Man in the Tinshop"!

For Uncle showed me "The Leader" there,
With his pale, bleak forehead and long, black hair;
Showed me the "Second," and "'Cello," and "Bass,"
And the "B-Flat," pouting and puffing his face
At the little end of the horn he blew
Silvery bubbles of music through;

And he coined me names of them, each in turn,
Some comical name that I laughed to learn,
Clean on down to the last and best,—
The lively little man, never at rest,
Who hides away at the end of the string,
And tinkers and plays on everything,—
    That 's "The Little Man in the Tinshop"!

Raking a drum like a rattle of hail,
Clinking a cymbal or castanet;
Chirping a twitter or sending a wail
Through a piccolo that thrills me yet;
Reeling ripples of riotous bells,
And tipsy tinkles of triangles—

Wrangled and tangled in skeins of sound
Till it seemed that my very soul spun round,
As I leaned, in a breathless joy, toward my
Radiant uncle, who snapped his eye
And said, with the courtliest wave of his hand,
"Why, that little master of all the band
Is The Little Man in the Tinshop!

"And I 've heard Verdi, the Wonderful,
And Paganini, and Ole Bull,
Mozart, Handel, and Mendelssohn,
And fair Parepa, whose matchless tone
Karl, her master, with magic bow,
Blent with the angels', and held her so

Tranced till the rapturous Infinite—
And I 've heard arias, faint and low,
From many an operatic light
Glimmering on my swimming sight
Dimmer and dimmer, until, at last,
I still sit, holding my roses fast
For The Little Man in the Tinshop."

Oho! my Little Man, joy to you—
And *yours*—and *theirs*—your lifetime through!
Though *I've* heard melodies, boy and man,
Since first "the show" of my life began,
Never yet have I listened to
Sadder, madder, or gladder glees
Than your unharmonied harmonies;

For yours is the music that appeals
To all the fervor the boy's heart feels—
All his glories, his wildest cheers,
His bravest hopes, and his brightest tears;
And so, with his first bouquet, he kneels
  To "The Little Man in the Tinshop."

FROM A BALLOON

Ho! we are loose. Hear how they shout,
And how their clamor dwindles out
Beneath us to the merest hum
Of earthly acclamation. Come,
Lean with me here and look below —
Why, bless you, man! don't tremble so!
There is no need of fear up here —
Not higher than the buzzard swings
About upon the atmosphere,
With drowsy eyes and open wings!
There, steady, now, and feast your eyes; —
See, we are tranced — we do not rise;
It is the earth that sinks from us:
But when I first beheld it thus,
And felt the breezes downward flow,
And heard all noises fail and die,
Until but silence and the sky
Above, around me, and below, —
Why, like you now, I swooned almost,
With mingled awe and fear and glee —
As giddy as an hour-old ghost
That stares into eternity.

"TRADIN' JOE"

I 'M one o' these cur'ous kind o' chaps
You think you know when you don't, perhaps!
I hain't no fool—ner I don't p'tend
To be so smart I could rickommend
Myself fer a *congerssman*, my friend!—
But I 'm kind o' betwixt-and-between, you know,—
One o' these fellers 'at folks calls "slow."
And I 'll say jest here I 'm kind o' queer
Regardin' things 'at I *see* and *hear*,—
Fer I 'm *thick* o' hearin' *sometimes*, and
It 's hard to git me to understand;
But other times it hain't, you bet!
Fer I don't sleep with both eyes shet!

I 've swopped a power in stock, and so
The neighbers calls me "Tradin' Joe"—
And I 'm goin' to tell you 'bout a trade,—
And one o' the best I ever made:

Folks has gone so fur 's to say
'At I 'm well fixed, in a *worldly* way,

And *bein'* so, and a *widower*,
It 's not su'prisin', as you 'll infer.
I 'm purty handy among the sect—
Widders especially, rickollect!
And I won't deny that along o' late
I 've hankered a heap fer the married state—
But some way o' 'nother the longer we wait
The harder it is to discover a mate.

Marshall Thomas,—a friend o' mine,
Doin' some in the tradin' line,
But a'most too *young* to know it all—
On'y at *picnics* er some *ball!*—
Says to me, in a banterin' way,
As we was a-loadin' stock one day,—
"You 're a-huntin' a wife, and I want you to see
My girl's mother, at Kankakee!—
She hain't over forty—good-lookin' and spry,
And jest the woman to fill your eye!
And I 'm a-goin' there Sund'y,—and now," says he,
"I want to take you along with *me;*
And you marry *her*, and," he says, "by 'shaw!
You 'll hev me fer yer son-in-law!"

I studied a while, and says I, "Well, I 'll
First have to see ef she suits my style;
And ef she does, you kin bet your life
Your mother-in-law will be my wife!"

Well, Sund'y come; and I fixed up some—
Putt on a collar—I did, by gum!—
Got down my "plug," and my satin vest—
(You would n't know me to see me dressed!—
But any one knows ef you got the clothes
You kin go in the crowd wher' the best of 'em goes!)
And I greeced my boots, and combed my hair
Keerfully over the bald place there;
And Marshall Thomas and me that day
Eat our dinners with Widder Gray
And her girl Han'! * * *

Well, jest a glance
O' the widder's smilin' countenance,
A-cuttin' up chicken and big pot-pies,
Would make a man hungry in Paradise!
And passin' p'serves and jelly and cake
'At would make an *angel's* appetite *ache!*—

Pourin' out coffee as yaller as gold—
Twic't as much as the cup could hold—
La! it was rich!—And then she 'd say,
"Take some o' *this!*" in her coaxin' way,
Tel ef I 'd been a hoss I 'd a-*foundered*, shore,
And jest dropped dead on her white-oak floor!

Well, the way I talked would a-done you good,
Ef you 'd a-been there to a-understood;
Tel I noticed Hanner and Marshall, they
Was a-noticin' me in a cur'ous way;
So I says to myse'f, says I, "Now, Joe,
The best thing fer you is to jest go slow!"
And I simmered down, and let them do
The bulk o' the talkin' the evening through.

And Marshall was still in a talkative gait
When we left, that evening—tollable late.
"How do you like her?" he says to me;
Says I, "She suits, to a 't-y-*Tee*'!"
And then I ast how matters stood
With him in the *opposite* neighberhood?
"Bully!" he says; "I ruther guess
I 'll finally git her to say the 'yes.'

I named it to her to-night, and she
Kind o' smiled, and said '*she 'd see*'—
And that 's a purty good sign!" says he:
"Yes," says I, "you 're ahead o' *me!*"
And then he laughed, and said, "*Go in!*"
And patted me on the shoulder ag'in.

Well, ever sence then I 've been ridin' a good
Deal through the Kankakee neighberhood;
And I make it convenient sometimes to stop
And hitch a few minutes, and kind o' drop
In at the widder's, and talk o' the crop
And one thing o' 'nother. And week afore last
The notion struck me, as I drove past,
I 'd stop at the place and state my case—
Might as well do it at first as last!

I felt first-rate; so I hitched at the gate,
And went up to the house; and, strange to relate,
Marshall Thomas had dropped in, *too.*—
"Glad to see you, sir, how do you do?"
He says, says he! Well—it *sounded queer;*
And when Han' told me to take a cheer,

Marshall got up and putt out o' the room—
And motioned his hand fer the *widder* to come.
I did n't say nothin' fer quite a spell,
But thinks I to myse'f, "Ther' 's a dog in the well!"
And Han' *she* smiled so cur'ous at me—
Says I, "What 's up?" And she says, says she,
"Marshall 's been at me to marry ag'in,
And I told him 'no,' jest as you come in."
Well, sumepin' o' 'nother in that girl's voice
Says to me, "Joseph, here 's your choice!"
And another minute her guileless breast
Was lovin'ly throbbin' ag'in my vest!—
And then I kissed her, and heerd a smack
Come like a' echo a-flutterin' back,
And we looked around, and in full view
Marshall was kissin' the widder too!
Well, we all of us laughed, in our glad su'prise,
Tel the tears come *a-streamin'* out of our eyes!
And when Marsh said " 'T was the squarest trade
That ever me and him had made,"
We both shuck hands, 'y jucks! and swore
We 'd stick together ferevermore.
And old 'Squire Chipman tuck us the trip:
And Marshall and me 's in pardnership!

UNCLE WILLIAM'S PICTURE

UNCLE WILLIAM, last July,
Had his picture took.
"Have it done, of course," says I,
"Jes' the way you look!"
(All dressed up, he was, fer the
Barbecue and jubilee
The old settlers helt.) So he —
Last he had it took.

Lide she 'd coaxed and begged and pled,
Sence her mother went;
But he 'd cough and shake his head
At all argyment;
Mebby clear his th'oat and say,
"What 's *my* likeness 'mount to, hey,
Now with *Mother* gone away
From us, like she went?"

But we projicked round, tel we
Got it figgered down

How we 'd git him, Lide and me,
  Drivin' into town;
Bragged how well he looked and fleshed
Up around the face, and freshed
With the morning air; and breshed
  His coat-collar down.

All so providential! W'y,
  Now he 's dead and gone,
Picture 'pears so lifelike I
  Want to start him on
Them old tales he ust to tell,
And old talks so sociable,
And old songs he sung so well—
  'Fore his voice was gone!

Face is sad to *Lide*, and they 's
  Sorrow in the eyes—
Kisses it sometimes, and lays
  It away and cries.
I smooth down her hair, and 'low
He is happy, anyhow,
Bein' there with Mother now,—
  Smile, and wipe my eyes.

THE FISHING-PARTY

Wunst we went a-fishin'—Me
An' my Pa an' Ma, all three,
When they wuz a picnic, 'way
Out to Hanch's Woods, one day.

An' they wuz a crick out there,
Where the fishes is, an' where
Little boys 't ain't big an' strong
Better have their folks along!

My Pa he ist fished an' fished!
An' my Ma she said she wished
Me an' her was home; an' Pa
Said he wished so worse 'n Ma.

Pa said ef you talk, er say
Anything, er sneeze, er play,
Hain't no fish, alive er dead,
Ever go' to bite! he said.

Purt'-nigh dark in town when we
Got back home; an' Ma, says she,
Now she 'll have a fish fer shore!
An' she buyed one at the store.

Nen at supper, Pa he won't
Eat no fish, an' says he don't
Like 'em.—An' he pounded me
When I choked! . . . Ma, did n't he?

SQUIRE HAWKINS'S STORY

I HAIN'T no hand at tellin' tales,
Er spinnin' yarns, as the sailors say;
Someway o' 'nother, language fails
To slide fer me in the oily way
That *lawyers* has; and I wisht it would,
Fer I 've got somepin' that I call good;
But bein' only a country squire,
I 've learned to listen and admire,
Ruther preferrin' to be addressed
Than talk myse'f—but I 'll do my best:—

Old Jeff Thompson—well, I 'll say,
Was the clos'test man I ever saw!—
Rich as cream, but the porest pay,
And the meanest man to work fer—La!
I 've knowed that man to work one "hand"—
Fer little er nothin', you understand—
From four o'clock in the morning light
Tel eight and nine o'clock at night,
And then find fault with his appetite!

He 'd drive all over the neighberhood
To miss the place where a toll-gate stood,
And slip in town, by some old road
That no two men in the county knowed,
With a jag o' wood, and a sack o' wheat,
That would n't burn and you could n't eat!
And the trades he 'd make, 'll I jest de-clare,
Was enough to make a preacher swear!
And then he 'd hitch, and hang about
Tel the lights in the toll-gate was blowed out,
And then the turnpike he 'd turn in
And sneak his way back home ag'in!

Some folks hint, and I make no doubt,
That that 's what wore his old wife out—
Toilin' away from day to day
And year to year, through heat and cold,
Uncomplainin'—the same old way
The martyrs died in the days of old;
And a-clingin', too, as the martyrs done,
To one fixed faith, and her *only* one,—
Little Patience, the sweetest child
That ever wept unrickonciled,

Er felt the pain and the ache and sting
That only a mother's death can bring.

Patience Thompson!—I think that name
Must a-come from a power above,
Fer it seemed to fit her jest the same
As a *gaiter* would, er a fine kid glove!
And to see that girl, with all the care
Of the household on her—I de-clare
It was *oudacious*, the work she 'd do,
And the thousand plans that she 'd putt through;
And sing like a medder-lark all day long,
And drownd her cares in the joys o' song;
And *laugh* sometimes tel the farmer's "hand,"
Away fur off in the fields, would stand
A-listenin', with the plow half drawn,
Tel the coaxin' echoes called him on;
And the furries seemed, in his dreamy eyes,
Like footpaths a-leadin' to Paradise,
As off through the hazy atmosphere
The call fer dinner reached his ear.

Now *love 's* as cunnin' a little thing
As a hummin'-bird upon the wing,

And as liable to poke his nose
Jest where folks would least suppose,—
And more 'n likely build his nest
Right in the heart you 'd leave unguessed,
And live and thrive at your expense—
At least, that 's *my* experience.
And old Jeff Thompson often thought,
In his se'fish way, that the quiet John
Was a stiddy chap, as a farm-hand *ought*
To always be,—fer the airliest dawn
Found John busy—and "*easy*," too,
Whenever his *wages* would fall due!—
To sum him up with a final touch,
He *eat* so little and *worked* so much,
That old Jeff laughed to hisse'f and said,
"He makes *me* money and airns his bread!"

But John, fer all of his quietude,
Would sometimes drap a word er so
That none but *Patience* understood,
And none but her was *meant* to know!—
Mayby at meal-times John would say,
As the sugar-bowl come down his way,

"Thanky, no; *my* coffee 's sweet
Enough fer *me!*" with sich conceit,
She 'd know at once, without no doubt,
He meant because *she* poured it out;
And smile and blush, and all sich stuff,
And ast ef it was "*strong* enough?"
And git the answer, neat and trim,
"It *could n't* be too 'strong' fer *him!*"

And so things went fer 'bout a year,
Tel John, at last, found pluck to go
And pour his tale in the old man's ear—
And ef it had been *hot lead*, I know
It could n't a-raised a louder fuss,
Ner a-riled the old man's temper wuss!
He jest *lit* in, and cussed and swore,
And lunged and rared, and ripped and tore,
And told John jest to leave his door,
And not to darken it no more!
But Patience cried, with eyes all wet,
"Remember, John, and don't ferget,
Whatever comes, I love you yet!"
But the old man thought, in his se'fish way,
"I 'll see her married rich some day;

And *that*," thinks he, "is money fer *me*—
And my will 's *law*, as it ought to be!"

So when, in the course of a month er so,
A *widower*, with a farm er two,
Comes to Jeff's, w'y, the folks, you know,
Had to *talk*—as the folks 'll do:
It was the talk of the neighberhood—
Patience and *John*, and *their* affairs;—
And this old chap with a few gray hairs
Had "cut John out," it was understood.
And some folks reckoned "Patience, too,
Knowed what *she* was a-goin' to do—
It was *like* her—la! indeed!—
All *she* loved was *dollars* and *cents*—
Like old Jeff—and they saw no need
Fer *John* to pine at *her* negligence!"

But others said, in a *kinder* way,
They missed the songs she used to sing—
They missed the smiles that used to play
Over her face, and the laughin' ring
Of her glad voice—that *everything*

Of her *old* se'f seemed dead and gone,
And this was the ghost that they gazed on!

Tel finally it was noised about
There was a *weddin'* soon to be
Down at Jeff's; and the "cat was out"
Shore enough!—'Ll the *Jee-mun-nee!*
It *riled* me when John told me so,—
Fer *I was* a *friend o' John's*, you know;
And his trimblin' voice jest broke in two—
As a feller's voice 'll sometimes do.—
And I says, says I, "Ef I know my biz—
And I think I know what *jestice* is,—
I 've read *some* law—and I 'd advise
A man like you to wipe his eyes,
And square his jaws and start *ag'in*,
Fer jestice is a-goin' to win!"
And it was n't long tel his eyes had cleared
As blue as the skies, and the *sun* appeared
In the shape of a good, old-fashioned smile
That I had n't seen fer a long, long while.

So we talked on fer a' hour er more,
And sunned ourselves in the open door,—

Tel a hoss-and-buggy down the road
Come a-drivin' up, that I guess John *knowed*,—
Fer he winked and says, "I 'll dessappear—
They 'd smell a mice ef they saw *me* here!"
And he thumbed his nose at the old gray mare,
And hid hisse'f in the house somewhere.

Well.—The rig drove up: and I raised my head
As old Jeff hollered to me and said
That "him and his old friend there had come
To see ef the squire was at home."
. . . I told 'em "I was; and I *aimed* to be
At every chance of a weddin'-fee!"
And then I laughed—and they laughed, too,—
Fer that was the object they had in view.
"Would I be on hands at eight that night?"
They ast; and 's-I, "You 're mighty right,
I 'll be on hands!" And then I bu'st
Out a-laughin' my very wu'st,—
And so did they, as they wheeled away
And drove to'rds town in a cloud o' dust.
Then I shet the door, and me and John
Laughed and *laughed*, and jest *laughed* on,

Tel Mother drapped her specs, and *by*
Jeewhillikers! I thought she 'd *die!*—
And she could n't a-told, I 'll bet my hat,
What on earth she was laughin' at!

But all o' the fun o' the tale hain't done!—
Fer a drizzlin' rain had jest begun,
And a-havin' 'bout four mile' to ride,
I jest concluded I 'd better light
Out fer Jeff's and save my hide,—
Fer *it was a-goin' to storm, that night!*
So we went down to the barn, and John
Saddled my beast, and I got on;
And he told me somepin' to not ferget,
And when I left, he was *laughin'* yet.

And, 'proachin' on to my journey's end,
The great big draps o' the rain come down,
And the thunder growled in a way to lend
An awful look to the lowerin' frown
The dull sky wore; and the lightnin' glanced
Tel my old mare jest *more 'n* pranced,
And tossed her head, and bugged her eyes
To about four times their natchurl size,

As the big black lips of the clouds 'ud drap
Out some oath of a thunder-clap,
And threaten on in an undertone
That chilled a feller clean to the bone!

But I struck shelter soon enough
To save myse'f. And the house was jammed
With the women-folks, and the weddin'-stuff:—
A great, long table, fairly *crammed*
With big pound-cakes—and chops and steaks—
And roasts and stews—and stumick-aches
Of every fashion, form, and size,
From twisters up to punkin-pies!
And candies, oranges, and figs,
And reezins,—all the "whilligigs"
And "jim-cracks" that the law allows
On sich occasions!—Bobs and bows
Of gigglin' girls, with corkscrew curls,
And fancy ribbons, reds and blues,
And "beau-ketchers" and "curliques"
To beat the world! And seven o'clock
Brought old Jeff;—and brought—*the groom*,—
With a sideboard-collar on, and stock
That choked him so, he had n't room

To *swaller* in, er even sneeze,
Er clear his th'oat with any ease
Er comfort—and a good square cough
Would saw his Adam's-apple off!

But as fer *Patience*—*My!* Oomh-*oomh!*—
I never saw her look so sweet!—
Her face was cream and roses, too;
And then them eyes o' heavenly blue
Jest made an angel all complete!
And when she split 'em up in smiles
And splintered 'em around the room,
And danced acrost and met the groom,
And *laughed out loud*—It kind o' spiles
My language when I come to that—
Fer, as she laid away his hat,
Thinks I, "*The papers hid inside*
Of that said hat must make a bride
A happy one fer all her life,
Er else a *wrecked* and *wretched wife!*"
And, someway, then, I thought of *John*,—
Then looked to'rds *Patience*. . . . She was *gone!*—
The door stood open, and the rain
Was dashin' in; and sharp and plain

Above the storm we heerd a cry—
A ringin', laughin', loud "Good-by!"
That died away, as fleet and fast
A hoss's hoofs went splashin' past!
And that was all. 'T was done that quick! . . .
You 've heerd o' fellers "lookin' sick"?
I wisht you 'd seen *the groom* jest then—
I wisht you 'd seen them two old men,
With starin' eyes that fairly *glared*
At one another, and the scared
And empty faces of the crowd,—
I wisht you could a-been allowed
To jest look on and see it all,—
And heerd the girls and women bawl
And wring their hands; and heerd old Jeff
A-cussin' as he swung hisse'f
Upon his hoss, who champed his bit
As though old Nick had holt of it:
And cheek by jowl the two old wrecks
Rode off as though they 'd break their necks.

And as we all stood starin' out
Into the night, I felt the brush

Of some one's hand, and turned about,
And heerd a voice that whispered, "*Hush!*—
They 're waitin' in the kitchen, and
You 're wanted. Don't you understand?"
Well, ef my *memory* serves me now,
I think I winked.—Well, anyhow,
I left the crowd a-gawkin' there,
And jest slipped off around to where
The back-door opened, and went in,
And turned and shet the door ag'in,
And mayby *locked* it—could n't swear,—
A woman's arms around me makes
Me liable to make mistakes.—
I read a marriage license nex',
But as I did n't have my specs
I jest *inferred* it was all right,
And tied the knot so mortal-tight
That Patience and my old friend John
Was safe enough from that time on!

Well now I might go on and tell
How all the joke at last leaked out,
And how the youngsters raised the yell
And rode the happy groom about

Upon their shoulders; how the bride
Was kissed a hunderd times beside
The one *I* give her,—tel she cried
And laughed untel she like to died!
I might go on and tell you all
About the supper—and the *ball.*—
You 'd ought to see me twist my heel
Through jest one old Furginny reel
Afore you die! er tromp the strings
Of some old fiddle tel she sings
Some old cowtillion, don't you know,
That putts the devil in yer toe!

We kep' the dancin' up tel *four*
O'clock, I reckon—mayby more.—
We hardly heerd the thunders roar,
Er *thought* about the *storm* that blowed—
And them two fellers on the road!
Tel all at onc't we heerd the door
Bu'st open, and a voice that *swore,*—
And old Jeff Thompson tuck the floor.
He shuck hisse'f and looked around
Like some old dog about half-drown'd—
His hat, I reckon, *weighed ten pound*

To say the least, and I 'll say, *shore*,
His *overcoat weighed fifty* more—
The wettest man you ever saw,
To have so dry a son-in-law!

He sized it all; and Patience laid
Her hand in John's, and looked afraid,
And waited. And a stiller set
O' folks, I *know*, you never met
In any court-room, where with dread
They wait to hear a verdick read.

The old man turned his eyes on me:
"And have you married 'em?" says he.
I nodded "Yes." "Well, that 'll do,"
He says, "and now we 're th'ough with *you*,—
You jest clear out, and I decide
And promise to be satisfied!"
He had n't nothin' more to say.
I saw, of course, how matters lay,
And left. But as I rode away
I heerd the roosters crow fer day.

DEAD SELVES

How many of my selves are dead?
The ghosts of many haunt me: Lo,
The baby in the tiny bed
With rockers on, is blanketed
And sleeping in the long ago;
And so I ask, with shaking head,
How many of my selves are dead?

A little face with drowsy eyes
And lisping lips comes mistily
From out the faded past, and tries
The prayers a mother breathed with sighs
Of anxious care in teaching me;
But face and form and prayers have fled—
How many of my selves are dead?

The little naked feet that slipped
In truant paths, and led the way
Through dead'ning pasture-lands, and tripped
O'er tangled poison-vines, and dipped
In streams forbidden—where are they?
In vain I listen for their tread—
How many of my selves are dead?

The awkward boy the teacher caught
Inditing letters filled with love,
Who was compelled, for all he fought,
To read aloud each tender thought
Of "Sugar Lump" and "Turtle Dove." . . .
I wonder where he hides his head—
How many of my selves are dead?

The earnest features of a youth
With manly fringe on lip and chin,
With eager tongue to tell the truth,
To offer love and life, forsooth,
So brave was he to woo and win;
A prouder man was never wed—
How many of my selves are dead?

The great, strong hands so all-inclined
To welcome toil, or smooth the care
From mother-brows, or quick to find
A leisure-scrap of any kind,
To toss the baby in the air,
Or clap at babbling things it said—
How many of my selves are dead?

The pact of brawn and scheming brain—
Conspiring in the plots of wealth,
Still delving, till the lengthened chain,
Unwindlassed in the mines of gain,
Recoils with dregs of ruined health
And pain and poverty instead—
How many of my selves are dead?

The faltering step, the faded hair—
Head, heart and soul, all echoing
With maundering fancies that declare
That life and love were never there,
Nor ever joy in anything,
Nor wounded heart that ever bled—
How many of my selves are dead?

So many of my selves are dead,
That, bending here above the brink
Of my last grave, with dizzy head,
I find my spirit comforted,
For all the idle things I think:
It can but be a peaceful bed,
Since all my other selves are dead.

IN SWIMMING-TIME

CLOUDS above, as white as wool,
  Drifting over skies as blue
As the eyes of beautiful
  Children when they smile at you;
Groves of maple, elm, and beech,
  With the sunshine sifted through
Branches, mingling each with each,
  Dim with shade and bright with dew;
Stripling trees, and poplars hoar,
Hickory and sycamore,
And the drowsy dogwood bowed
Where the ripples laugh aloud,
And the crooning creek is stirred
  To a gaiety that now
Mates the warble of the bird
  Teetering on the hazel-bough;
Grasses long and fine and fair
As your schoolboy sweetheart's hair,

Backward roached and twirled and twined
By the fingers of the wind;
Vines and mosses, interlinked
  Down dark aisles and deep ravines,
Where the stream runs, willow-brinked,
  Round a bend where some one leans
Faint and vague and indistinct
  As the like reflected thing
  In the current shimmering.
Childish voices farther on,
Where the truant stream has gone,
Vex the echoes of the wood
Till no word is understood,
Save that one is well aware
Happiness is hiding there.
There, in leafy coverts, nude
  Little bodies poise and leap,
Spattering the solitude
And the silence everywhere—
  Mimic monsters of the deep!
Wallowing in sandy shoals—
  Plunging headlong out of sight;
  And, with spurtings of delight,
Clutching hands, and slippery soles,

Climbing up the treacherous steep
Over which the spring-board spurns
Each again as he returns.
Ah! the glorious carnival!
Purple lips and chattering teeth—
Eyes that burn—but, in beneath,
Every care beyond recall,
Every task forgotten quite—
And again, in dreams at night,
Dropping, drifting through it all!

SONG OF THE BULLET

It whizzed and whistled along the blurred
  And red-blent ranks; and it nicked the star
Of an epaulette, as it snarled the word—
                                        War!

On it sped—and the lifted wrist
  Of the ensign-bearer stung, and straight
Dropped at his side as the word was hissed—
                                        Hate!

On went the missile—smoothed the blue
  Of a jaunty cap and the curls thereof,
Cooing, soft as a dove might do—
                                        Love!

Sang!—sang on!—sang hate—sang war—
  Sang love, in sooth, till it needs must cease,
Hushed in the heart it was questing for.—
                                        Peace!

DEAD, MY LORDS

DEAD, my lords and gentlemen!—
Stilled the tongue, and stayed the pen;
Cheek unflushed and eye unlit—
Done with life, and glad of it.

Curb your praises now as then:
Dead, my lords and gentlemen.—
What he wrought found its reward
In the tolerance of the Lord.

Ye who fain had barred his path,
Dread ye now this look he hath?—
Dead, my lords and gentlemen—
Dare ye not smile back again?

Low he lies, yet high and great
Looms he, lying thus in state.—
How exalted o'er ye when
Dead, my lords and gentlemen!

HOME AGAIN

I 'M bin a-visitun 'bout a week
To my little Cousin's at Nameless Creek;
An' I 'm got the hives an' a new straw hat,
An' I 'm come back home where my beau lives at.

A SEA-SONG FROM THE SHORE

HAIL! Ho!
Sail! Ho!
Ahoy! Ahoy! Ahoy!
Who calls to me,
So far at sea?
Only a little boy!

Sail! Ho!
Hail! Ho!
The sailor he sails the sea:
I wish he would capture a little sea-horse
And send him home to me.

I wish, as he sails
Through the tropical gales,
He would catch me a sea-bird, too,
With its silver wings
And the song it sings,
And its breast of down and dew!

I wish he would catch me a
Little mermaid,
Some island where he lands,
With her dripping curls,
And her crown of pearls,
And the looking-glass in her hands!

Hail! Ho!
Sail! Ho!
Sail far o'er the fabulous main!
And if I were a sailor,
I 'd sail with you,
Though I never sailed back again.

A BOY'S MOTHER

My Mother she 's so good to me,
Ef I wuz good as I could be,
I could n't be as good — no, *sir!* —
Can't *any* boy be good as *her!*

She loves me when I 'm glad er sad;
She loves me when I 'm good er bad;
An', what 's a funniest thing, she says
She loves me when she punishes.

I don't like her to punish me.—
That don't hurt,—but it hurts to see
Her cryin'.—Nen *I* cry; an' nen
We *both* cry an' be good again.

She loves me when she cuts an' sews
My little cloak an' Sund'y clothes;
An' when my Pa comes home to tea,
She loves him most as much as me.

She laughs an' tells him all I said,
An' grabs me up an' pats my head;
An' I hug her, an' hug my Pa,
An' love him purt'-nigh much as Ma.

THE RUNAWAY BOY

WUNST I sassed my Pa, an' he
Won't stand that, an' punished me,—
Nen when he wuz gone that day,
I slipped out an' runned away.

I tooked all my copper-cents,
An' clumbed over our back fence
In the jimpson-weeds 'at growed
Ever'where all down the road.

Nen I got out there, an' nen
I runned some—an' runned again,
When I met a man 'at led
A big cow 'at shooked her head.

I went down a long, long lane
Where wuz little pigs a-play'n';
An' a grea'-big pig went "*Booh!*"
An' jumped up, an' skeered me too.

Nen I scampered past, an' they
Was somebody hollered "*Hey!*"
An' I ist looked ever'where,
An' they wuz nobody there.

I *want* to, but I 'm 'fraid to try
To go back. . . . An' by-an'-by
Somepin' hurts my th'oat inside—
An' I want my Ma—an' cried.

Nen a grea'-big girl come through
Where 's a gate, an' telled me who
Am I? an' ef I tell where
My home 's at she 'll show me there.

But I could n't ist but tell
What 's my *name;* an' she says "well,"
An' ist tooked me up an' says
"She know where I live, she guess."

Nen she telled me hug wite close
Round her neck!—an' off she goes
Skippin' up the street! An' nen
Purty soon I 'm home again.

An' my Ma, when she kissed me,
Kissed the big girl too, an' *she*
Kissed me—ef I p'omise shore
I won't run away no more!

THE SPOILED CHILD

'CAUSE Herbert Graham 's a' only child—
"Wuz I there, Ma?"
His paruntz uz got him purt'-nigh spiled—
"Wuz I there, Ma?"
Allus ever'where his Ma tells
Where *she 's* bin at, little Herbert yells,
"Wuz I there, Ma?"
An' when she telled us wunst when she
Wuz ist 'bout big as him an' me,
W'y, little Herbert he says, says-ee,
"Wuz I there, Ma?"
Foolishest young-un you ever saw.—
"*Wuz I there, Ma? Wuz I there, Ma?*"

THE KIND OLD MAN

THE kind old man—the mild old man—
  Who smiled on the boys at play,
Dreaming, perchance, of his own glad youth
  When he was as blithe and gay!

And the larger urchin tossed the ball,
  And the lesser held the bat—
Though the kindly old man's eyes were blurred
  He could even notice that!

But suddenly he was shocked to hear
  Words that I dare not write,
And he hastened, in his kindly way,
  To curb them as he might!

And he said, "Tut! tut! you naughty boy
With the ball! for shame!" and then,
"You boy with the bat, whack him over the head
If he calls you that again!"

The kind old man—the mild old man—
Who gazed on the boys at play,
Dreaming, perchance, of his own wild youth
When he was as tough as they!

THE BOY LIVES ON OUR FARM

THE Boy lives on our Farm, he 's not
  Afeard o' horses none!
An' he can make 'em lope, er trot,
  Er rack, er pace, er run.
Sometimes he drives *two* horses, when
  He comes to town an' brings
A wagonful o' 'taters nen,
  An' roastin'-ears an' things.

Two horses is "a team," he says,—
  An' when you drive er hitch,
The *right* un 's a "near-horse," I guess,
  Er "off"—I don't know which.—
The Boy lives on our Farm, he told
  Me, too, 'at he can see,
By lookin' at their teeth, how old
  A horse is, to a T!

I 'd be the gladdest boy alive
  Ef I knowed much as that,
An' could stand up like him an' drive,
  An' ist push back my hat,
Like he comes skallyhootin' through
  Our alley, with one arm
A-wavin' Fare-ye-well! to you—
  The Boy lives on our Farm!

THE DOODLE-BUGS'S CHARM

WHEN Uncle Sidney he comes here—
  An' Fred an' me an' Min,—
My Ma she says she bet you yet
  The roof 'll tumble in!
Fer Uncle he ist *romps* with us:
  An' wunst, out in our shed,
He telled us 'bout the Doodle-Bugs,
  An' what they 'll do, he said,
Ef you 'll ist holler "Doodle-Bugs!"—
  Out by our garden-bed—
"Doodle-Bugs! Doodle-Bugs!
  Come up an' git some bread!"

Ain't Uncle Sidney funny man?—
  " He 's childish 'most as me"—
My Ma sometimes she tells him that—
  " He ac's so foolishly!"
W'y, wunst, out in our garden-path,
  Wite by the pie-plant bed,
He all sprawled out there in the dirt
  An' ist scrooched down his head,

An' "Doodle! Doodle! Doodle-Bugs!"
  My Uncle Sidney said,—
" Doodle-Bugs! Doodle-Bugs!
  Come up an' git some bread!"

An' nen he showed us little holes
  All bored there in the ground,
An' little weenty heaps o' dust
  'At 's piled there all around:
An' Uncle said, when he 's like us,
  Er purt'-nigh big as Fred,
That wuz the Doodle-Bugs's Charm —
  To call 'em up, he said:—
"Doodle! Doodle! Doodle-Bugs!"
  An' they 'd poke out their head—
"Doodle-Bugs! Doodle-Bugs!
  Come up an' git some bread!"

LITTLE COUSIN JASPER

Little Cousin Jasper, he
Don't live in this town, like me,—
He lives 'way to Rensselaer,
An' ist comes to visit here.

He says 'at our courthouse-square
Ain't nigh big as theirn is there!—
He says their town 's big as four
Er five towns like this, an' more!

He says ef his folks moved here
He 'd cry to leave Rensselaer—
'Cause they 's prairies there, an' lakes,
An' wile-ducks an' rattlesnakes!

Yes, 'n' little Jasper's Pa
Shoots most things you ever saw!—
Wunst he shot a deer, one day,
'At swummed off an' got away.

Little Cousin Jasper went
An' camped out wunst in a tent
Wiv his Pa, an' helt his gun
While he kilt a turrapun.

An' when his Ma heerd o' that,
An' more things his Pa 's bin at,
She says, "Yes, 'n' he 'll git shot
'Fore he 's man-grown, like as not!"

An' they 's mussrats there, an' minks,
An' di-dippers, an' chee-winks,—
Yes, 'n' cal'mus-root you chew
All up an' 't 'on't pizen you!

An', in town, 's a flag-pole there—
Highest one 'at 's anywhere
In this world!—wite in the street
Where the big mass-meetin's meet.

Yes, 'n' Jasper he says they
Got a brass band there, an' play
On it, an' march up an' down
An' all over round the town!

Wisht our town ain't like it is!—
Wisht it 's ist as big as his!
Wisht 'at *his* folks they 'd move *here,*
An' *we 'd* move to Rensselaer!

GIVE ME THE BABY

GIVE me the baby to hold, my dear—
  To hold and hug, and to love and kiss.
Ah! he will come to me, never a fear—
  Come to the nest of a breast like this,
As warm for him as his face with cheer.
Give me the baby to hold, my dear!

Trustfully yield him to my caress.
  "Bother," you say? What! "a bother" to *me?*—
To fill up my soul with such happiness
  As the love of a baby that laughs to be
Snuggled away where my heart can hear!
Give me the baby to hold, my dear!

Ah, but his hands are grimed, you say,
  And would soil my laces and clutch my hair.—
Well, what would pleasure me more, I pray,
  Than the touch and tug of the wee hands there?—
The wee hands there, and the warm face here—
Give me the baby to hold, my dear!

Give me the baby! (Oh, won't you see?
  . . . Somewhere, out where the green of the lawn
Is turning to gray, and the maple-tree
  Is weeping its leaves of gold upon
A little mound, with a dead rose near. . . .)
Give me the baby to hold, my dear!

THE BEE-BAG

WHEN I was ist a Brownie — a weenty-teenty Brownie —
Long afore I got to be like Childerns is to-day,—
My good old Brownie granny gimme sweeter thing 'an can'y —
An' 'at 's my little bee-bag the Fairies stold away!
O my little bee-bag —
My little funny bee-bag —
My little honey bee-bag
The Fairies stold away!

One time when I bin swung in wiv annuver Brownie young-un
An' lef' sleepin' in a pea-pod while our parunts went to play,
I waked up ist a-cryin' an' a-sobbin' an' a-sighin'
Fer my little funny bee-bag the Fairies stold away!
O my little bee-bag—
My little funny bee-bag—
My little honey bee-bag
The Fairies stold away!

It 's awful much bewilder'n', but 'at 's why I 'm *a Childern*,
Ner goin' to git to be no more a Brownie sence that day!
My parunts, so imprudent, lef' me sleepin' when they should n't!
An' I want my little bee-bag the Fairies stold away!
O my little bee-bag—
My little funny bee-bag—
My little honey bee-bag
The Fairies stold away!

LITTLE MARJORIE

"Where is little Marjorie?"
There 's the robin in the tree,
With his gallant call once more
From the boughs above the door!
There 's the bluebird's note, and there
Are spring-voices everywhere
Calling, calling ceaselessly—
"Where is little Marjorie?"

And her old playmate, the rain,
Calling at the window-pane
In soft syllables that win
Not her answer from within—

"Where is little Marjorie?"—
 Or is it the rain, ah me!
 Or wild gusts of tears that were
 Calling us—not calling her!

"Where is little Marjorie?"
 Oh, in high security
 She is hidden from the reach
 Of all voices that beseech:
 She is where no troubled word,
 Sob or sigh is ever heard,
 Since God whispered tenderly—
"Where is little Marjorie?"

THE TRULY MARVELOUS

GIUNTS is the biggest mens they air
In all this world er anywhere!—
An' Tom Thumb he 's the most little-est man,
'Cause wunst he lived in a oyshture-can!

'MONGST THE HILLS O' SOMERSET

'MONGST the Hills o' Somerset
Wisht I was a-roamin' yet!
My feet won't get usen to
These low lands I 'm trompin' through.
Wisht I could go back there, and
Stroke the long grass with my hand,
Kind o' like my sweetheart's hair
Smoothed out underneath it there!
Wisht I could set eyes once more
On our shadders, on before,
Climbin', in the airly dawn,
Up the slopes 'at love growed on
Natchurl as the violet
'Mongst the Hills o' Somerset!

20

How 't 'u'd rest a man like me
Jest fer 'bout an hour to be
Up there where the morning air
Could reach out and ketch me there!—
Snatch my breath away, and then
Rensh and give it back again
Fresh as dew, and smellin' of
The old pinks I ust to love,
And a-flavor'n' ever' breeze
With mixt hints o' mulberries
And May-apples, from the thick
Bottom-lands along the crick
Where the fish bit, dry er wet,
'Mongst the Hills o' Somerset!

Like a livin' pictur' things
All comes back: the bluebird swings
In the maple, tongue and bill
Trillin' glory fit to kill!
In the orchard, jay and bee
Ripens the first pears fer me,
And the "Prince's Harvest" they
Tumble to me where I lay

In the clover, provin' still
"A boy's will is the wind's will."
Clean fergot is time, and care,
And thick hearin', and gray hair—
But they 's nothin' I ferget
'Mongst the Hills o' Somerset!

Middle-aged—to be edzact,
Very middle-aged, in fact,—
Yet a-thinkin' back to then,
I 'm the same wild boy again!
There 's the dear old home once more,
And there 's Mother at the door—
Dead, I know, fer thirty year',
Yet she 's singin', and I hear;
And there 's Jo, and Mary Jane,
And Pap, comin' up the lane!
Dusk 's a-fallin'; and the dew,
'Pears like, it 's a-fallin' too—
Dreamin' we 're all livin' yet
'Mongst the Hills o' Somerset!

OLD JOHN HENRY

OLD John 's jes' made o' the commonest stuff—
Old John Henry—
He 's tough, I reckon,—but none too tough—
Too tough though 's better than not enough!
Says old John Henry.
He does his best, and when his best 's bad,
He don't fret none, ner he don't git sad—
He simply 'lows it 's the best he had:
Old John Henry!

His doctern 's jes' o' the plainest brand—
Old John Henry—
A smilin' face and a hearty hand
'S religen 'at all folks understand,
Says old John Henry.

He 's stove up some with the rhumatiz,
And they hain't no shine on them shoes o' his,
And his hair hain't cut — but his eye-teeth is:
Old John Henry!

He feeds hisse'f when the stock 's all fed —
Old John Henry —
And sleeps like a babe when he goes to bed —
And dreams o' heaven and home-made bread,
Says old John Henry.
He hain't refined as he 'd ort to be
To fit the statutes o' poetry,
Ner his clothes don't fit him — but *he* fits *me*:
Old John Henry!

MY FIRST SPECTACLES

At first I laughed—for it was quite
  An oddity to see
My reflex looking from the glass
  Through spectacles at me.

But as I gazed I really found
  They so improved my sight
That many wrinkles in my face
  Were mixed with my delight;

And many streaks of silver, too,
  Were gleaming in my hair,
With quite a hint of baldness that
  I never dreamed was there.

And as I readjusted them
  And winked in slow surprise,
A something like a mist had come
  Between them and my eyes.

And, peering vainly still, the old
  Optician said to me,
The while he took them from my nose
  And wiped them hastily:

"Jest now, of course, your eyes is apt
  To water some—but where
Is any man's on earth that won't
  The first he has to wear?"

SCOTTY

SCOTTY 's dead.— Of course he is!
Jes' that same old luck of his!—
Ever sence we went cahoots
He 's be'n first, you bet yer boots!
When our schoolin' first begun,
Got two whippin's to my one:
Stold and smoked the first cigar:
Stood up first before the bar,
Takin' whisky-straight—and me
Wastin' time on "blackberry"!
Beat me in the Army, too,
And clean on the whole way through!—
In more scrapes around the camp,
And more troubles, on the tramp:
Fought and fell there by my side
With more bullets in his hide,

And more glory in the cause,—
That 's the kind o' man *he* was!
Luck liked Scotty more 'n me.—
I got married: Scotty, he
Never even would *apply*
Fer the pension-money I
Had to beg of "Uncle Sam"—
That 's the kind o' cuss *I* am!—
Scotty allus first and best—
Me the last and ornriest!
Yit fer all that 's said and done—
All the battles fought and won—
We hain't prospered, him ner me—
Both as pore as pore could be,—
Though we 've allus, up tel now,
Stuck together anyhow—
Scotty allus, as I 've said,
Luckiest—And now he 's *dead!*

MY WHITE BREAD

DEM good old days done past and gone
In old Ca'line wha I wuz bo'n
W'en my old Misst'ess she fust said,
  "Yo 's a-eatin' yo' white bread!"
Oh, dem 's de times uts done gone by
W'en de nights shine cla, an' de coon clim' high,
An' I sop my soul in 'possum-pie,
  Das a-eatin' my white bread!

Its dem 's de nights ut I cross my legs
An' pat de flo' ez I twis' de pegs
O' de banjo up twil de gals all said,
  "Yo 's a-eatin' yo' white bread!"

Oh, dem 's de times ut I usen fo' to blow
On de long reeds cut in de old by-o,
An' de frogs jine in like dey glad fo' to know
    I 's a-eatin' my white bread.

An' I shet my eyes fo' to conjuh up
Dem good ole days ut fills my cup
Wid de times ut fust ole Misst'ess said,
    "Yo 's a-eatin' yo' white bread!"
Oh, dem 's de dreams ut I fines de best;
An' bald an' gray ez a hornet's nest,
I drap my head on de good Lord's breast,
    Says a-eatin' my white bread!

BACK FROM TOWN

OLD friends allus is the best,
Halest-like and heartiest:
Knowed us first, and don't allow
We 're so blame much better now!
They was standin' at the bars
When we grabbed "the kivvered kyars"
And lit out fer town, to make
Money—and that old mistake!

We thought then the world we went
Into beat "The Settlement,"
And the friends 'at we 'd make there
Would beat any anywhere!—
And they *do*—fer that 's their biz:
They beat all the friends they is—
'Cept the raal old friends like you
'At staid home, like *I 'd* ort to!

W'y, of all the good things yit
I ain't shet of, is to quit
Business, and git back to sheer
These old comforts waitin' here—
These old friends; and these old hands
'At a feller understands;
These old winter nights, and old
Young-folks chased in out the cold!

Sing "Hard Times 'll come ag'in
No More!" and neighbers all jine in!
Here 's a feller come from town
Wants that-air old fiddle down
From the chimbly!—Git the floor
Cleared fer one cowtillion more!—
It 's poke the kitchen-fire, says he,
And shake a friendly leg with me!

A MAN BY THE NAME OF BOLUS

A MAN by the name of Bolus — (all 'at we 'll ever know
Of the stranger's name, I reckon — and I 'm kind o' glad it 's so!) —
Got off here, Christmas morning, looked 'round the town, and then
Kind o' sized up the folks, I guess, and — went away again!

The fac's is, this man Bolus got "run in," Christmas-day;
The town turned out to see it, and cheered, and blocked the way;
And they dragged him 'fore the Mayor — fer he could n't er *would n't* walk —
And socked him down fer trial — though he could n't er *would n't* talk!

Drunk? They was no doubt of it!—W'y, the marshal
of the town
Laughed and testified 'at he fell *up*-stairs 'stid o' *down!*
This man by the name of Bolus?—W'y, he even
drapped his jaw
And snored on through his "hearin'"—drunk as you
ever saw!

One feller spit in his boot-leg, and another 'n' drapped
a small
Little chunk o' ice down his collar,—but he did n't
wake at all!
And they all nearly split when his Honor said, in one
of his witty ways,
To "chalk it down fer him, 'Called away—be back
in thirty days!'"

That 's where this man named Bolus slid, kind o' like
in a fit,
Flat on the floor; and—drat my ears! I hear 'em
a-laughin' yit!
Somebody fetched Doc Sifers from jest acrost the
hall—
And all Doc said was, "Morphine! We 're too late!"
and that 's all!

That 's how they found his name out—piece of a letter
'at read:
"Your wife has lost her reason, and little Nathan 's
dead—
Come ef you kin,—fergive *her*—but, Bolus, as fer *me*,
This hour I send a bullet through where my heart *ort*
to be!"

Man by the name of Bolus!—As his revilers broke
Fer the open air, 'peared-like, to me, I heerd a voice
'at spoke—
*Man by the name of Bolus! git up from where you
lay—
Git up and smile white at 'em, with your hands crossed
thataway!*

OLD CHUMS

"If I die first," my old chum paused to say,
"Mind! not a whimper of regret;—instead,
Laugh and be glad, as I shall.—Being dead,
I shall not lodge so very far away
But that our mirth shall mingle.—So, the day
The word comes, joy with me." "I 'll try," I said,
Though, even speaking, sighed and shook my head
And turned, with misted eyes. His roundelay
Rang gaily on the stair; and then the door
Opened and—closed. . . . Yet something of the clear,
Hale hope, and force of wholesome faith he had
Abided with me—strengthened more and more.—
Then—then they brought his broken body here:
And I laughed—whisperingly—and we were glad.

WHAT A DEAD MAN SAID

HEAR what a dead man said to me.
His lips moved not, and the eyelids lay
Shut as the leaves of a white rose may
Ere the wan bud blooms out perfectly;
And the lifeless hands they were stiffly crossed
As they always cross them over the breast
When the soul goes nude and the corpse is dressed;
And over the form, in its long sleep lost,
From forehead down to the pointed feet
That peaked the foot of the winding-sheet,
Pallid patience and perfect rest.—
It was the voice of a dream, may be,
But it seemed that the dead man said to me:
"I, indeed, am the man that died
Yesternight—and you weep for this;

But, lo, I am with you, side by side,
As we have walked when the summer sun
Made the smiles of our faces one,
And touched our lips with the same warm kiss.
Do not doubt that I tell you true—
I am the man you once called friend,
And caught my hand when I came to you,
And loosed it only because the end
Of the path I walked of a sudden stopped—
And a dead man's hand must needs be dropped—
And I—though it 's strange to think so now—
I have wept, as you weep for me,
And pressed hot palms to my aching brow
And moaned through the long night ceaselessly.
Yet have I lived to forget my pain,
As you will live to be glad again—
Though never so glad as this hour am I,
Tasting a rapture of delight
Vast as the heavens are infinite,
And dear as the hour I came to die.
Living and loving, I dreamed my cup
Brimmed sometimes, and with marvelings
I have lifted and tipped it up
And drank to the dregs of all sweet things.

Living, 't was but a *dream* of bliss—
Now I *realize* all it is;
And now my only shadow of grief
Is that I may not give relief
Unto those living and dreaming on,
And woo them graveward, as I have gone,
And show death's loveliness,—for they
Shudder and shrink as they walk this way,
Never dreaming that all they dread
Is their purest delight when dead."

Thus it was, or it seemed to be,
That the voice of the dead man spoke to me.

CUORED O' SKEERIN'

'LISH, you rickollect that-air
Dad-burn skittish old bay mare
Was no livin' with!—'at skeerd
'T ever'thing she seed er heerd!—
Th'owed 'Ves' Anders, and th'owed Pap,
First he straddled her—*k-slap!*—
And Izory—well!—th'owed *her*
Hain't no tellin' jest how fur!—
Broke her collar-bone—and might
Jest 'a' kilt the gyrl outright!

Course I 'd heerd 'em make their boast
She th'ow any feller, 'most,
Ever topped her! S' I, "I know
One man 'at she 'll never th'ow!"

So I rid her in to mill,
And, jest comin' round the hill,
Met a *traction-engine!*— Ort
Jest 'a' heerd that old mare snort,
And lay back her yeers, and see
Her a-tryin' to th'ow *me!*
Course I never said a word,
But thinks I, "My ladybird,
You 'll git cuored, right here and now,
Of yer dy-does anyhow!"

So I stuck her — tel she 'd jest
Done her very level best;
Then I slides off — strips the lines
Over her fool-head, and finds
Me a little saplin'-gad,
'Side the road: — And there we had
Our own fun! — jest wore her out!
Mounted her, and faced about,
And jest made her *nose* that-air
Little traction-engine there!

YOUR VIOLIN

YOUR violin! Ah me!
'T was fashioned o'er the sea,
In storied Italy—
What matter where?
It is its voice that sways
And thrills me as it plays
The airs of other days—
The days that were!

Then let your magic bow
Glide lightly to and fro.—
I close my eyes, and so,
In vast content,
I kiss my hand to you,
And to the tunes we knew
Of old, as well as to
Your instrument!

Poured out of some dim dream
Of lulling sounds that seem

Like ripples of a stream
  Twanged lightly by
The slender, tender hands
Of weeping-willow wands
That droop where gleaming sands
  And pebbles lie.

A melody that swoons
In all the truant tunes
Long listless afternoons
  Lure from the breeze,
When woodland boughs are stirred,
And moaning doves are heard,
And laughter afterward
  Beneath the trees.

Through all the chorusing,
I hear on leaves of spring
The drip and pattering
  Of April skies,
With echoes faint and sweet
As baby-angel feet
Might wake along a street
  Of Paradise.

TO A SKULL

TURN your face this way;
I 'm not weary of it—
Every hour of every day
More and more I love it—
Grinning in that jolly guise
Of bare bones and empty eyes!

Was this hollow dome,
Where I tap my finger,
Once the spirit's narrow home—
Where you loved to linger,
Hiding, as to-day are we,
From the self-same destiny?

O'er and o'er again
Have I put the query—
Was existence so in vain
That you look so cheery?—

Death of such a benefit
That you smile, possessing it?

Did your throbbing brow
  Tire of all the flutter
Of such fancyings as now
  You, at last, may utter
In that grin so grimly bland
Only death can understand?

Has the shallow glee
  Of old dreams of pleasure
Left you ever wholly free
  To float out, at leisure,
O'er the shoreless, trackless trance
Of unsounded circumstance?

Only this I read
  In your changeless features,—
You, at least, have gained a meed
  Held from living creatures:
You have naught to ask.—Beside,
You do grin so satisfied!

A VISION OF SUMMER

'T WAS a marvelous vision of Summer.—
  That morning the dawn was late,
And came, like a long dream-ridden guest,
  Through the gold of the Eastern gate.

Languid it came, and halting,
  As one that yawned, half roused,
With lifted arms and indolent lids
  And eyes that drowsed and drowsed.

A glimmering haze hung over
  The face of the smiling air;
And the green of the trees and the blue of the leas
  And the skies gleamed everywhere.

And the dewdrops' dazzling jewels,
  In garlands and diadems,
Lightened and twinkled and glanced and shot
  As the glints of a thousand gems:

Emeralds of dew on the grasses;
  The rose with rubies set;
On the lily, diamonds; and amethysts
  Pale on the violet.

And there were the pinks of the fuchsias,
  And the peony's crimson hue,
The lavender of the hollyhocks,
  And the morning-glory's blue:

The purple of the pansy bloom,
  And the passionate flush of the face
Of the velvet-rose; and the thick perfume
  Of the locust every place.

The air and the sun and the shadows
  Were wedded and made as one;
And the winds ran over the meadows
  As little children run:

And the winds poured over the meadows
  And along the willowy way
The river ran, with its ripples shod
  With the sunshine of the day:

O the winds flowed over the meadows
  In a tide of eddies and calms,
And the bared brow felt the touch of it
  As a sweetheart's tender palms.

And the lark went palpitating
  Up through the glorious skies,
His song spilled down from the blue profound
  As a song from Paradise.

And here was the loitering current—
  Stayed by a drift of sedge
And sodden logs—scummed thick with the gold
  Of the pollen from edge to edge.

The catbird piped in the hazel,
  And the harsh kingfisher screamed,
And the crane, in amber and oozy swirls,
  Dozed in the reeds and dreamed.

And in through the tumbled driftage
  And the tangled roots below,
The waters warbled and gurgled and lisped
  Like the lips of long ago.

And the senses caught, through the music,
Twinkles of dabbling feet,
And glimpses of faces in coverts green,
And voices faint and sweet.

And back from the lands enchanted
Where my earliest mirth was born,
The trill of a laugh was blown to me
Like the blare of an elfin horn.

Again I romped through the clover;
And again I lay supine
On grassy swards, where the skies, like eyes,
Looked lovingly back in mine.

And over my vision floated
Misty illusive things—
Trailing strands of the gossamer
On heavenward wanderings:

Figures that veered and wavered,
Luring the sight, and then
Glancing away into nothingness,
And blinked into shape again.

From out far depths of the forest,
  Ineffably sad and lorn,
Like the yearning cry of a long-lost love,
  The moan of the dove was borne.

And through lush glooms of the thicket
  The flash of the redbird's wings
On branches of star-white blooms that shook
  And thrilled with its twitterings.

Through mossy and viny vistas,
  Soaked ever with deepest shade,
Dimly the dull owl stared and stared
  From his bosky ambuscade.

And up through the rifted tree-tops
  That signaled the wayward breeze,
I saw the hulk of the hawk becalmed
  Far out on the azure seas.

Then sudden an awe fell on me,
  As the hush of the golden day
Rounded to noon, as a May to June
  That a lover has dreamed away.

And I heard, in the breathless silence,
  And the full, glad light of the sun,
The tinkle and drip of a timorous shower—
  Ceasing as it begun.

And my thoughts, like the leaves and grasses
  In a rapture of joy and pain,
Seemed fondled and petted and beat upon
  With a tremulous patter of rain.

BEREAVED

Let me come in where you sit weeping,—aye,
Let me, who have not any child to die,
Weep with you for the little one whose love
        I have known nothing of.

The little arms that slowly, slowly loosed
Their pressure round your neck; the hands you used
To kiss.—Such arms—such hands I never knew.
        May I not weep with you?

Fain would I be of service—say some thing,
Between the tears, that would be comforting,—
But ah! so sadder than yourselves am I,
        Who have no child to die.

A SONG OF THE CRUISE

O THE sun and the rain, and the rain and the sun!
There 'll be sunshine again when the tempest is done;
And the storm will beat back when the shining is past—
But in some happy haven we 'll anchor at last.
Then murmur no more,
In lull or in roar,
But smile and be brave till the voyage is o'er.

O the rain and the sun, and the sun and the rain!
When the tempest is done, then the sunshine again;
And in rapture we 'll ride through the stormiest gales,
For God's hand 's on the helm and His breath in the sails.
Then murmur no more,
In lull or in roar,
But smile and be brave till the voyage is o'er.

THE DEAD WIFE

Always I see her in a saintly guise
  Of lilied raiment, white as her own brow
When first I kissed the teardrops to the eyes
      That smile forever now.

Those gentle eyes! They seem the same to me,
  As, looking through the warm dews of mine own,
I see them gazing downward patiently
      Where, lost and all alone

In the great emptiness of night, I bow
  And sob aloud for one returning touch
Of the dear hands that, Heaven having now,
      I need so much—so much!

SOMEDAY

SOMEDAY:—So many tearful eyes
Are watching for thy dawning light;
So many faces toward the skies
Are weary of the night!

So many failing prayers that reel
And stagger upward through the storm,
And yearning hands that reach and feel
No pressure true and warm.

So many hearts whose crimson wine
Is wasted to a purple stain
And blurred and streaked with drops of brine
Upon the lips of Pain.

Oh, come to them!—these weary ones!
Or if thou still must bide a while,
Make stronger yet the hope that runs
Before thy coming smile:

And haste and find them where they wait—
Let summer-winds blow down that way,
And all they long for, soon or late,
Bring round to them, Someday.

CLOSE THE BOOK

CLOSE the book, and leave the tale
All unfinished. It is best:
Brighter fancy will not fail
To relate the rest.

We have read it on and on,
Till each character, in sooth,
By the master-touches drawn,
Is a living truth.

Leave it so, and let us sit,
With the volume laid away—
Cut no other leaf of it,
But as Fancy may.—

Then the friends that we have met
In its pages will endure,
And the villain, even yet,
May be white and pure.

Close the book, and leave the tale
All unfinished. It is best:
Brighter fancy will not fail
To relate the rest.

www.ingramcontent.com/pod-product-compliance
Lightning Source LLC
LaVergne TN
LVHW011226110826
845150LV00006B/1557

* 9 7 8 1 4 2 5 5 1 5 2 2 5 *